Whoopie Pies

70 delectably different recipes shown step by step,
with 200 photographs

MOWIE KAY
With photography by Nicki Dowey

LORENZ BOOKS

This edition is published by Lorenz Books,
an imprint of Anness Publishing Ltd,
Blaby Road, Wigston, Leicestershire LE18 4SE

Email: info@anness.com

Web: www.lorenzbooks.com; www.annesspublishing.com

If you like the images in this book and would like to
investigate using them for publishing, promotions or
advertising, please visit our website www.practicalpictures.com
for more information.

Publisher: Joanna Lorenz
Editor: Kate Eddison
Photographer: Nicki Dowey
Food stylist: Lucy McKelvie
Prop stylist: Wei Tang
Designer: Lisa Tai
Production controller: Bessie Bai

PUBLISHER'S NOTE

ETHICAL TRADING POLICY

At Anness Publishing we believe that business should be
conducted in an ethical and ecologically sustainable way, with
respect for the environment and a proper regard to the
replacement of the natural resources we employ.

As a publisher, we use a lot of wood pulp in high-quality paper for
printing, and that wood commonly comes from spruce trees. We
are therefore currently growing more than 750,000 trees in three
Scottish forest plantations: Berrymoss (130 hectares/320 acres),
West Touxhill (125 hectares/305 acres) and Deveron Forest
(75 hectares/185 acres). The forests we manage contain more than
3.5 times the number of trees employed each year in making
paper for the books we manufacture.

Because of this ongoing ecological investment programme, you,
as our customer, can have the pleasure and reassurance of
knowing that a tree is being cultivated on your behalf to naturally
replace the materials used to make the book you are holding.

Our forestry programme is run in accordance with the UK
Woodland Assurance Scheme (UKWAS) and will be certified by
the internationally recognized Forest Stewardship Council (FSC).
The FSC is a non-government organization dedicated to
promoting responsible management of the world's forests.
Certification ensures forests are managed in an environmentally
sustainable and socially responsible way. For further information
about this scheme, go to www.annesspublishing.com/trees

NOTES

Bracketed terms are intended for American readers.

For all recipes, quantities are given in both metric and imperial
measures and, where appropriate, in standard cups and spoons.
Follow one set of measures, but not a mixture, because they are
not interchangeable.

Standard spoon and cup measures are level. 1 tsp = 5ml,
1 tbsp = 15ml, 1 cup = 250ml/8fl oz.

Australian standard tablespoons are 20ml. Australian readers
should use 3 tsp in place of 1 tbsp for measuring small quantities.

American pints are 16fl oz/2 cups. American readers should use
20fl oz/2.5 cups in place of 1 pint when measuring liquids.

Electric oven temperatures in this book are for conventional ovens.
When using a fan oven, the temperature will probably need to be
reduced by about 10–20°C/20–40°F. Since ovens vary, you should
check with your manufacturer's instruction book for guidance.

The nutritional analysis given for each recipe is calculated per
portion (i.e. serving or item), unless otherwise stated. If the recipe
gives a range, such as Serves 4–6, then the nutritional analysis
will be for the smaller portion size, i.e. 6 servings. The analysis
does not include optional ingredients, such as salt added to taste.

Medium (US large) eggs are used unless otherwise stated.

Main front cover image shows Chilli and Chocolate Whoopie Pies,
Cream Soda Whoopie Pies, Coconut and Lemon Whoopie
Wedding Stack, Ginger Lychee Whoopie Pies, and Pistachio Rose
Water Whoopie Pies – for recipes, see pages 76, 80, 94, 74 and 72.

Contents

Introduction

Whoopie pies are considered to be an American creation, specifically a New England phenomenon, created to use up leftover cake mixture. It is thought that when the Amish found one of these treats in their lunch boxes, they would shout 'whoopie!' True or not, the name is now famous worldwide.

WHAT IS A WHOOPIE PIE?

Shaped like a burger, bigger and easier to make than macarons, and rapidly taking over from the cupcake as the kings of the baking world, whoopie pies are here to stay. A whoopie pie, at its most basic level, consists of two round 'cakes' that are sandwiched together with a soft filling. They can be flavoured with an endless array of delicious ingredients, and decorated with all sorts of toppings, from melted chocolate to creamy icings.

The original and best-known whoopie pie is wonderful in its simplicity: rich chocolate cakes with sticky marshmallow filling. Today, however, the range of cakes, fillings and toppings is seemingly infinite, demonstrating the versatility of this scrummy treat, and lending itself to mixing and matching cakes, fillings and toppings.

Below Coloured icings and pretty decorations give extra character to your whoopie pie creations, and look fabulous when served as a contrasting selection.

Above Varied sizes of whoopie pie are suitable for different occasions and any recipe can be adapted to make either mini, regular or large pies. Minis are great for kids' parties!

The cake mixture tends to be made using milk or buttermilk, and each whoopie pie maker has his or her preferences. In this book, buttermilk is the main liquid ingredient in the cakes as it results in a superior flavour, as well as making the cakes stay moist for longer. Buttermilk adds a richness to the whoopie pie cakes that you don't get in a simple cupcake.

ALL KINDS OF WHOOPIE PIES

Whoopie pies can be made in an almost limitless medley of flavours, sizes, shapes and colours. The original and standard whoopie pie is large enough to eat with two hands, as if biting into a burger. Once you have mastered making a basic whoopie, you can experiment with pretty much every aspect of the recipe. Try making them into mini whoopies or even into a giant whoopie cake! Fillings include, but are not limited to, marshmallow, buttercream and whipped cream, and each one can be augmented

Right Use the collar of a loose-bottomed cake tin (pan) to guide the cake mixture into a giant whoopie pie cake: a simple technique with really effective results.

with sumptuous colours and intriguing flavours. Create special occasion whoopies by going to town on toppings: drizzle them decadently with chocolate, decorate them beautifully with icing, or brush them elegantly with a fruity glaze.

HOW TO USE THIS BOOK

Packed with an astounding 70 recipes, this book is a treasure trove of whoopie pie ideas and you are sure to find a multitude of recipes perfect for any occasion. However, once you have got the hang of whoopies, you do not have to feel restricted to specific recipes. Feel free to mix and match cake recipes with fillings and toppings – be creative! There are lots of ideas for pretty decorations, and once you start shopping you will find a plethora of wonderful sprinkles, glitters, colourings and much more. Try specialist cake shops or online retailers for all the latest decorative ideas. You can also change the sizes, if you like. This book gives 3 basic sizes – regular, mini and giant – and the same amount of filling is used for each. You just need to change the amount of mixture you pipe or spoon out – simple!

WHOOPIE PIE SIZES

The standard-sized whoopie pies are big enough to hold in both hands like a burger. The cakes are piped on to baking sheets in 5cm/2in rounds, but they can spread in the oven depending on the type of cake mixture. Mini whoopies are piped into 3cm/1¼in rounds and require roughly half the mixture for each cake. Therefore, the same recipe will make double the amount of minis. You can also make a giant whoopie pie cake, perfect for birthdays, using a 24cm/9½in cake tin (pan) as a guide. The same amount of mixture will make 1 giant whoopie, 12 regular whoopies or 24 mini whoopies, so it is simple to adapt the recipes to make whichever size you require. Mini whoopie pie cakes will need a reduced cooking time, and giant cakes will need a bit longer in the oven.

Left There are a multitude of ways to inject your individual style into your whoopie pies, such as decoratively dusting them with icing (confectioners') sugar using a paper doily.

Whoopie pie ingredients

Only a small number of basic and inexpensive ingredients are needed for a simple whoopie pie, but with a little imagination a vast range of tastes and textures can be brought together in a limitless array of innovative and tasty whoopie pies.

Flour The most common flour used in the whoopie pie cakes is plain (all-purpose) flour. It is a soft, white wheat flour with no added raising agents. Self-raising (self-rising) flour has raising agents already added. It needs to be used within 6 months as, once opened, the raising agents lose some of their qualities. Gluten-free flour is used by those with a gluten intolerance. Gluten is what gives cakes their texture, so something needs to be added to replace it, such as xanthan gum.

Buttermilk A main ingredient in most cake mixtures in this book, buttermilk is sour and low in fat, and is the liquid (whey) obtained from the butter-churning process.

Milk Used in combination with buttermilk, milk is sometimes added to create a more pliable batter. Use full cream (whole) milk if possible.

Below Buttermilk and milk are used in most of the cake mixtures in this book.

Cream Double (heavy) cream is whipped with sugar to form one of the simplest and most elegant fillings. It is also used to soften the textures of buttercreams. Whipping cream can be used when a lighter filling is required.

Butter A main ingredient in cakes and buttercreams, unsalted butter is usually used. Soften it beforehand.

Sugar Caster (superfine) sugar is granulated (white) sugar that has been pulverized into fine granules. It is used in cake mixtures and fillings. Icing (confectioners') sugar has been ground to a very fine powder. It is dusted over finished whoopies or made into a glaze. Soft light brown sugar is a moist, dense sugar with a mild molasses flavour.

Eggs Use free range eggs, if possible, for a superior flavour. Eggs in this book are medium (US large).

Below Whipped cream makes a tasty filling that is simple to achieve.

MAKING BUTTERMILK
Buttermilk is readily available in supermarkets, but if you cannot find it, an effective substitute can be made by adding 15ml/1 tbsp lemon juice to 250ml/8fl oz/ 1 cup full cream (whole) milk. Stir, then allow the mixture to stand for 5 minutes before using.

Raising agents When using plain flour for making the cakes, you will also need a raising agent. Bicarbonate of soda is the most common agent in this book. It is an alkaline powder that produces carbon dioxide, which you see as tiny air bubbles in the cakes. Xanthan gum is used to replace the gluten in gluten-free flours.

Vanilla The seeds of vanilla pods (beans) are used in the cakes, to give a rich taste and speckled appearance.

Below Eggs are a basic ingredient in almost every cake mixture.

*Above **Dark chocolate can be melted for the simplest of toppings.***

*Above **The amount of food colouring you need to use depends on its type.***

*Above **Perfect for a decadent finish, edible gold leaf is extremely delicate.***

A very good alternative is vanilla paste, which is a syrupy mixture containing vanilla seeds. You could also use vanilla extract. Vanilla essence, however, is not recommended as it is a synthetic-tasting, inferior substitute.

Cocoa powder (unsweetened) is used in chocolate cakes and fillings. It is the portion of cocoa solids remaining after the cocoa butter has been removed.

Chocolate Dark (bittersweet) chocolate contains a minimum of 70% cocoa solids, and is the best choice for creating rich, chocolatey cakes. Milk, white and plain (semi-sweet) chocolates are also utilized in fillings and toppings. They can be made into a luxurious ganache or simply melted over finished whoopies.

Honey Clear (runny) honey is used in buttercreams, cake mixtures or simply on its own as a sticky topping. It is also used in place of sugar to add natural sweetness and flavour.

Golden (light corn) syrup Like honey, this is used instead of sugar. It is also used in marshmallow fillings. Light corn syrup is best for giving the

whiteness to marshmallow, but it is difficult to find in the UK, so golden syrup can be used instead. Although it won't be perfectly white, it will taste just as nice!

Fruit Use fresh fruit in season for the best flavour. Many types of fruit can be chopped up in fillings or used as pretty toppings. They can also be made into jams or fruit curds for fillings. Various fruit juices can be used for flavouring cakes and buttercreams, and can be mixed with icing (confectioners') sugar to make sweet glazes. Citrus rinds can be grated and used for flavouring or decorating. Dried fruits should not be stored for too long; they need to be succulent and juicy for the best flavour and texture.

Spices Warming and comforting, spices are a must for many seasonal recipes. Ground spices will last for up to 6 months; after that, they will lose some of their flavour.

Nuts and seeds Ground, flaked (sliced) or whole, nuts and seeds add texture and taste to whoopie pies. Recipes include almonds, hazelnuts, walnuts, poppy seeds and peanuts.

Food colourings There are different types of food colouring. Gels are ideal because you only need a small amount, but they are not always available in supermarkets, so traditional liquids are used in most of the recipes.

Cheeses For rich and indulgent fillings, there is nothing better than cream cheese. It is soft and mild so it combines well with a wide range of other flavours. Mascarpone is a soft, mild Italian triple-cream cheese made from crème fraîche, and is often used in desserts.

Decorative ingredients There is no limit to the possibilities when it comes to finishing touches. Edible glitter is a mixture of gum arabic and water, spread thinly as a liquid gel, allowed to harden, then cut into tiny pieces. Sprinkle on to whoopies for sparkle. Gold leaf adds elegance when placed on the top of whoopies. It is very fragile and is best handled with tweezers. Sprinkles come in endless colours, shapes and sizes. Sprinkle them on top of whoopies while the icing is still wet so the sprinkles stick. Alternatively, roll the whoopies in the sprinkles so they stick to the edge of the filling.

Essential equipment

Bakers are only as good as their tools and it is recommended that you invest in good quality baking equipment, if you can. You only need a few essentials to start baking whoopie pies; the rest you can acquire as you get more experienced.

Baking trays Most ovens already come with one or more baking trays, and these are usually acceptable for baking, but it is always best to invest in at least one good quality baking tray that is flat and not curved at the edge. A good baking tray diffuses heat more equally across its surface. You will need at least two baking trays for the recipes in this book, depending on their size. If you cannot fit all the cakes on your baking trays, cook them in batches.

Baking parchment Used for lining baking trays, baking parchment is inexpensive. You can also buy siliconized baking parchment, which is silicone-coated on both sides, and provides a perfect non-stick surface for baking without having to grease trays or parchment. You can re-use it a few times, so it is worth the extra expense.

Silicone mats Made from fibreglass and silicone, these mats can be used instead of baking parchment and can be re-used thousands of times. To clean, simply wash them in soapy water, rinse and allow them to dry. They save time and, in the long run, money, and are environmentally friendly as they create less waste. If you intend to bake a lot of whoopies, it is worth investing in these.

Piping bags and nozzles Made of plastic, fabric or polyester, piping bags are the ultimate tool in achieving perfectly round whoopie pie cakes. With a bit of practice, you'll be piping perfect rounds with ease. Most bags are re-usable and fit a range of nozzles. Large, plain round nozzles are best for piping cake mixture (batter) on to baking trays. Smaller, star-shaped nozzles are useful for piping filling and decorating the tops.

Whoopie pie tins (pans) A new invention, whoopie pie tins are available in most baking stores. They were created solely for making whoopie pies. They are a simple, practical idea, which work as a great alternative to piping. They create evenly sized whoopie pies with very straight edges, so although they help you to make uniform cakes, they do not give the characteristic slopes of the classic whoopie.

Ice cream scoops Due to the thick consistency of whoopie pie cake mixture, an ice cream scoop can be the most practical way of making whoopie pie cakes. Hemispherical in shape, some are fitted with a mechanical release that drops a perfect round of cake mixture on to the baking trays, and are invaluable if you are not confident with a piping bag, or for nutty cake mixtures.

Below Lining your baking tray with baking parchment or silicone mats makes it easy to remove cooked cakes.

Below Piping is not easy at first, but once you have got the hang of it, it is the best way to create pretty effects.

Below Using spoons or ice cream scoops is another way of forming the whoopie pie cakes on baking trays.

Electric food mixer An invaluable piece of equipment that allows you to mix and add ingredients hands-free, an electric food mixer is a time-saving investment that should last many years. They are also useful for making marshmallow filling. If you do not have one, a mixing bowl and an electric hand whisk will do the job.

Electric hand whisk Useful in combination with an electric food mixer, an electric hand whisk allows you to make fillings at the same time as the cake mixtures are mixing in the food mixer. These are also perfect for making buttercreams and whipping cream. Although more labour-intensive, a balloon whisk can often be used instead.

Scales It is best to invest in digital scales for precise measurements.

Sieve (strainer) This is essential for sifting flour into cake mixtures and for sifting icing (confectioners') sugar or cocoa powder when making smooth icings or buttercreams. It is best to have two separate ones for dry and wet ingredients.

Below It is important to sift flour before adding it to cake mixtures, to add some air and remove lumps.

Above An electric hand whisk will make short work of beating cake mixtures or whipping cream.

Pastry brush Useful for brushing glazes on to the tops of whoopies, pastry brushes are available in many types, shapes and sizes. Silicone brushes are a good choice as they withstand heat, rinse easily and last much longer, with the added bonus of not losing any bristles.

Cooling racks When whoopie pie cakes come out of the oven, they should be transferred to a wire rack and allowed to cool.

Below Allow whoopie pie cakes to cool completely before adding the filling and decorating them.

Above A palette knife will help you to achieve a professional look when applying toppings to your whoopies.

Palette knife or metal spatula These tools are perfect for smoothing or creating peaks in icing or buttercream. Palette knives and metal spatulas are also useful for transferring baked whoopie pie cakes from baking trays on to cooling racks.

Pastry (cookie) cutters It is easy to form different whoopie pie shapes by pouring the cake mixture into a Swiss roll tin (jelly roll pan), baking it, then using pastry cutters to cut out shapes.

Below Heart-shaped cutters are a fabulous idea for Valentine's Day, but you could try other shapes too.

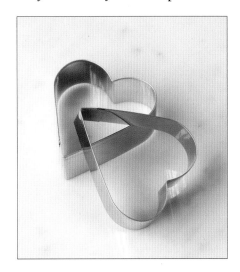

Tips and techniques

There are a few techniques to get to grips with when making whoopie pies, such as decorative piping and making marshmallow filling, but once you have mastered a few tricks of the trade, you will be whipping up whoopies time and time again.

PREPARING THE CAKE MIXTURE (BATTER)

The whoopie pie cake mixture is quite a forgiving and versatile batter that allows for small changes and mistakes; a little more or less flour or buttermilk won't ruin it. The quickest way to make the cake mixture is to use an electric food mixer, though you must fold in the dry ingredients by hand. You can always make the cake mixture using an electric hand whisk, or a simple wooden spoon. The mixture should have a thick consistency: when a spatula in the mixture is lifted, the batter should tear with clear-cut edges. If it drips off the spatula, it is too runny and needs more flour.

FORMING THE CAKES

You should be able to fit 12 regular-sized whoopie pie cakes on to each baking tray, but if not, just use more baking trays. Bake them in batches, if you need to. It is important to space the cakes 5cm/2in apart as once placed in the oven, the batter expands rapidly before rising. The recipes in this book use a piping bag to form the cakes, but there are multiple ways of doing this. Give them all a try and see which method suits you best.

Using a piping (pastry) bag This technique gives equal, well-rounded whoopie pies. Use a large piping bag fitted with a large plain nozzle; fill the piping bag with the cake mixture, hold it vertically over the baking trays and pipe the rounds. The trick is to squeeze the same amount of mixture for each cake, then stop squeezing and quickly lift the piping bag away.

Using two tablespoons Scoop a tablespoon of cake mixture with one tablespoon and use a second spoon to scrape it on to the baking tray.

Using an ice cream scoop Fill the scoop, then, using the release trigger, allow the batter to slide on to the baking tray. This is useful if the mixture contains nuts and is difficult to pipe.

Using a pastry (cookie) cutter Place a 5cm/2in plain round pastry cutter on the baking tray, fill with a tablespoon of cake mixture, flatten with the back of the spoon and lift the cutter off. Only round cutters can be used this way as the mixture spreads out in the oven. To create different shapes, cook all the mixture in a Swiss roll tin (jelly roll pan) and, once cool, punch out shapes using pastry cutters.

Using a whoopie pie tin (pan) Simply spoon an even amount of mixture into each 'cup' to give uniform shapes. You will need two whoopie pie tins, or alternatively you can make the cakes in two batches.

Below An electric hand whisk is an invaluable labour-saving tool when it comes to making cake mixtures.

Below Piping whoopie pie cakes is a skill that can be mastered easily with a little practice.

Below For a simple, fuss-free method, form your whoopie pie cakes using an ice cream scoop.

BAKING TIMES AND TEMPERATURES

When it comes to any form of baking, the best advice is to know your oven. Oven temperatures vary from one oven to the next, and temperatures within each oven vary from top to bottom, depending on the origin of heat. An oven thermometer is a very good investment. Place this on the same level as the baking tray before the baking tray goes into the oven to get an accurate reading. It is also best to clear the ovens of all baking trays and racks while preheating and baking, and to only have the trays of whoopie pies in the oven during baking. This helps heat distribution and reduces oven preheating times.

The bigger the whoopie pie cakes, the longer they need to bake. For the minis, this is around 10–12 minutes, for the normal size it is around 12–15 minutes, and for the giant cakes it is between 20–30 minutes. The best way to test if a cake is ready is to press it gently. If it bounces back, it is ready to take out of the oven; if it doesn't bounce back it means it is still raw in the middle, and if it doesn't give when pressed, then it has been in too long.

Below Allow whoopie pie cakes to cool completely before filling and topping them.

MAKING MARSHMALLOW FILLINGS

The classic marshmallow filling appears in many recipes and is surprisingly easy to make. It is best to use an electric food mixer to make it, but you can use a mixing bowl and an electric hand whisk if you do not have one. It is too thick and sticky to use a balloon whisk. Due to its stickiness, piping can be difficult and very messy, so spooning it on to the cakes is usually the best option. Grease your spoon with a little oil to prevent the marshmallow from sticking. It is best to spoon it on to the cakes immediately, as the gelatine starts to set once left to stand. You can always buy marshmallow fluff, for an instant marshmallow, if you like.

MELTING CHOCOLATE

Chocolate should always be melted in a heatproof bowl set over a pan of simmering water. Ensure that the bowl doesn't touch the water, as if the temperature is too high it will result in a grainy consistency.

Below Melt chocolate over a pan of gently simmering water, if possible, stirring until it is smooth.

STORAGE

Whoopie pies are generally best served on the day you make them, but they can be made in advance. Although moist when initially baked, the cakes can dry out very quickly if not stored correctly. You can make the cakes and fillings in advance, if you like, and store them both separately until ready to assemble. Alternatively, just make the cakes in advance and make the filling fresh on the day of serving. Wrap the cakes in clear film (plastic wrap) or store them in an airtight container for up to 5 days.

You could also assemble the whoopies (without their toppings) in advance. To allow them to retain their moisture, wrap the whoopies in clear film. If the filling has fresh cream in it, you will need to store them in the refrigerator for up to 2–3 days. For marshmallow and other fillings that do not need to be chilled, store them in an airtight container for up to 5 days. Once you are ready to serve them, bring any chilled whoopies to room temperature, then add the topping. Serve immediately.

Below It takes a bit of practice to get to grips with sticky marshmallow filling, but the results are worth it.

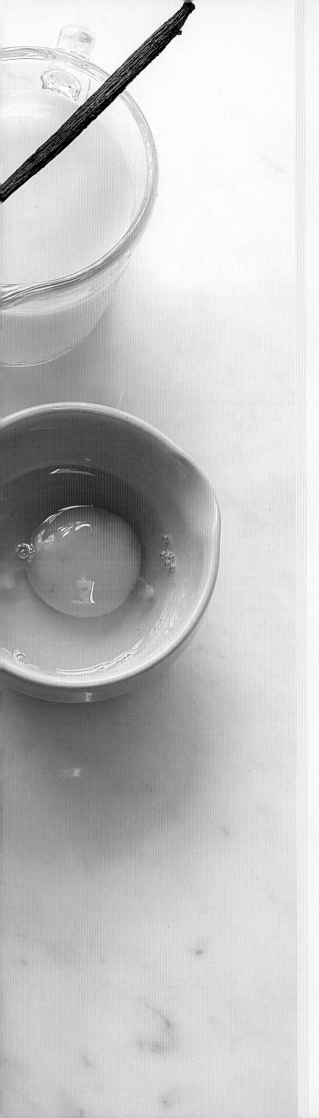

Classic whoopies

These classic whoopie pies embody all that we love about comfort food and easy baking. They include the most famous whoopies, such as Red Velvet Whoopie Pie and the original chocolate whoopie with marshmallow filling, The Classic. They all make an indulgent treat with a pot of steaming tea or a mug of cocoa or coffee. Although they might be the most famous of flavour combinations, which have stood the test of time, don't be afraid to mix and match fillings with cake flavours. Experiment and enjoy!

The classic

This is the original and classic whoopie pie recipe – two rich chocolate cakes sandwiched together with a light and fluffy marshmallow filling. Pure indulgence. Ideally, you will need an electric food mixer to make the marshmallow, although you could use an electric whisk.

MAKES 12 WHOOPIE PIES

For the cakes
125g/4¼oz/8½ tbsp unsalted
  butter, softened
90g/3½oz/scant ½ cup soft light
  brown sugar
90g/3½oz/½ cup caster
  (superfine) sugar
1 egg
seeds of 1 vanilla pod (bean)
300g/11oz/2¾ cups plain
  (all-purpose) flour
50g/2oz unsweetened cocoa powder
7.5ml/1½ tsp bicarbonate of soda
  (baking soda)
5ml/1 tsp salt
250ml/8fl oz/1 cup milk

For the marshmallow filling
50ml/2fl oz/¼ cup boiling water
15ml/1 tbsp powdered gelatine
175g/6oz/generous ¾ cup caster
  (superfine) sugar
75ml/2½fl oz/⅓ cup golden
  (light corn) syrup
25ml/1½ tbsp cold water

1 Preheat the oven to 180°C/350°F/ Gas 4. Line two baking trays with baking parchment or silicone mats.

2 To make the cakes, place the butter and sugars in a bowl and beat together until light and creamy. Beat in the egg, then stir in the vanilla seeds until fully incorporated.

3 In a separate bowl, sift the flour with the cocoa powder, bicarbonate of soda and salt. Fold half of the dry ingredients into the butter mixture. Mix in the milk, then mix in the remainder of the dry ingredients.

4 Using a piping (pastry) bag fitted with a large plain nozzle, pipe 12 5cm/ 2in rounds of cake mixture (batter) 5cm/2in apart on each baking tray. Bake for 8–10 minutes, or until the cakes bounce back when gently pressed. Transfer to a wire rack to cool.

5 For the filling, put the boiling water in the bowl of an electric mixer and sprinkle with the gelatine. Whisk on low speed until the gelatine dissolves. In a pan, heat the sugar, golden syrup and cold water, stirring, until the mixture comes to a rolling boil. With the mixer on low, gradually add the hot syrup. Turn the mixer to high and whisk for 5 minutes, until the mixture turns very thick, pale and fluffy.

6 Using an oiled spoon, drop a large dollop of marshmallow on to the flat side of one cake, then top with the flat side of another and gently squeeze them together. Repeat to make 12 pies.

Nutritional information: Energy 327kcal/1384kJ; Protein 5g; Carbohydrate 57g, of which sugars 37g; Fat 11g, of which saturates 7g; Cholesterol 45mg; Calcium 78mg; Fibre 0.9g; Sodium 379mg.

Red velvet whoopie pies

Red velvet is a classic American cake, deep red in colour, which forms the basis of these show-stopping whoopie pies. Gel food colouring works better than other food colouring types and only a teaspoonful is needed to achieve the desired deep red effect.

MAKES 12 WHOOPIE PIES

For the cakes
125g/4¼oz/8½ tbsp unsalted
  butter, softened
175g/6oz/¾ cup soft light brown sugar
seeds of 1 vanilla pod (bean)
1 egg
300g/11oz/2¾ cups plain
  (all-purpose) flour
50g/2oz unsweetened cocoa powder
7.5ml/1½ tsp bicarbonate of soda
  (baking soda)
5ml/1 tsp salt
250ml/8fl oz/1 cup buttermilk
5ml/1 tsp red food colouring

For the marshmallow filling
50ml/2fl oz/¼ cup boiling water
15ml/1 tbsp powdered gelatine
175g/6oz/generous ¾ cup caster
  (superfine) sugar
75ml/2½fl oz/⅓ cup golden
  (light corn) syrup
25ml/1½ tbsp cold water

1 Preheat the oven to 180°C/350°F/ Gas 4. Line two baking trays with baking parchment or silicone mats.

2 Beat the butter, sugar and vanilla until light and creamy. Beat in the egg.

3 In a separate bowl, sift the flour with the cocoa powder, bicarbonate of soda and salt. In a measuring jug (cup), mix the buttermilk and food colouring. Fold half of the dry ingredients into the butter mixture. Mix in the buttermilk mixture, then the rest of the dry ingredients. Using a piping (pastry) bag fitted with a large plain nozzle, pipe 12 5cm/2in rounds of mixture (batter) 5cm/2in apart on each baking tray.

4 Bake for 12–15 minutes, or until the cakes bounce back when gently pressed. Transfer to a wire rack to cool.

5 For the filling, put the boiling water in the bowl of an electric mixer and sprinkle with the gelatine. Whisk on low speed until the gelatine dissolves. In a pan, heat the sugar, golden syrup and cold water, stirring, until the mixture comes to a rolling boil. With the mixer on low, gradually add the hot syrup. Turn the mixer to high and whisk for 5 minutes, until the mixture turns very thick, pale and fluffy.

6 Using an oiled tablespoon, place a tablespoonful of the marshmallow on to the flat side of one cake and top with the flat side of another. Repeat to make 12 pies.

Nutritional information: Energy 325kcal/1376kJ; Protein 5g; Carbohydrate 57g, of which sugars 37g; Fat 10g, of which saturates 6g; Cholesterol 44mg; Calcium 78mg; Fibre 0.9g; Sodium 382mg.

Mini chocolate chip whoopie pies

A chocolate lover's delight, these dense and complex whoopie pies are interspersed with luxurious dark chocolate chips and sandwiched together with a sinful but light chocolate buttercream. Try decorating the pies with chocolate shavings instead of cocoa powder.

2 For the cakes, beat the butter, sugar and vanilla seeds until creamy. Beat in the egg. In a separate bowl, sift the flour with the bicarbonate of soda and salt, then stir in the chocolate. Fold half of the flour mixture into the butter mixture. Mix in the buttermilk, then the remainder of the flour mixture.

3 Using a piping (pastry) bag fitted with a large plain nozzle, pipe 24 3cm/1¼in rounds of cake mixture (batter) 4cm/½in apart on each of the baking trays. Bake for 10–12 minutes, or until the cakes bounce back when gently pressed. Transfer to a wire rack to cool.

4 For the filling, place the icing sugar, vanilla seeds and butter in a bowl. Using an electric whisk on medium speed, whisk until crumbly. Slowly whisk in the cream, then increase the speed to high and whisk until creamy and smooth. Fold in the sifted cocoa powder and chocolate chips.

5 Using a piping bag fitted with a star-shaped nozzle, pipe some filling on to the flat side of one cake and top with the flat side of another. Repeat to make 24 pies. Dust with cocoa powder.

MAKES 24 WHOOPIE PIES

For the cakes
125g/4¼oz/8½ tbsp unsalted butter, softened
175g/6oz/¾ cup soft light brown sugar
seeds of 1 vanilla pod (bean)
1 egg
325g/11½oz/scant 3 cups plain (all-purpose) flour
7.5ml/1½ tsp bicarbonate of soda (baking soda)
5ml/1 tsp salt
100g/3¾oz dark (bittersweet) chocolate, chopped into chunks
250ml/8fl oz/1 cup buttermilk

For the buttercream filling
300g/11oz/2¾ cups icing (confectioners') sugar
seeds of 1 vanilla pod (bean)
150g/5oz/10 tbsp unsalted butter, softened
90ml/6 tbsp double (heavy) cream
50g/2oz unsweetened cocoa powder
40g/1½oz plain (semisweet) chocolate chips

unsweetened cocoa powder, for dusting

1 Preheat the oven to 180°C/350°F/ Gas 4. Line two baking trays with baking parchment or silicone mats.

Nutritional information: Energy 273kcal/1151kJ; Protein 3g; Carbohydrate 35g, of which sugars 24g; Fat 15g, of which saturates 9g; Cholesterol 42mg; Calcium 48mg; Fibre 0.5g; Sodium 217mg.

Mini marble cake whoopie pies

Nothing beats a classic marble cake with its swirls of chocolate throughout the vanilla. These whoopie pies use the same technique for a beautiful marbled pattern. They are very moist and moreish, and their mini size means that you can feel less guilty about munching more than one!

MAKES 24 WHOOPIE PIES

For the cakes
130g/4½oz/generous ½ cup
   unsalted butter, softened
150g/5oz/¾ cup caster
   (superfine) sugar
seeds of 1 vanilla pod (bean)
1 egg
325g/11½oz/scant 3 cups plain
   (all-purpose) flour
7.5ml/1½ tsp bicarbonate of soda
   (baking soda)
5ml/1 tsp salt
50ml/2fl oz/¼ cup milk
150ml/¼ pint/⅔ cup buttermilk
25g/1oz unsweetened cocoa powder

For the buttercream filling
300g/11oz/2¾ cups icing
   (confectioners') sugar
seeds of 1 vanilla pod (bean)
150g/5oz/10 tbsp unsalted butter,
   softened
90ml/6 tbsp double (heavy) cream
25g/1oz unsweetened cocoa powder

For the topping
150g/5oz dark (bittersweet)
   chocolate, melted

1 Preheat the oven to 180°C/350°F/ Gas 4. Line two baking trays with baking parchment or silicone mats.

2 To make the cakes, place the butter, sugar and vanilla seeds in a bowl and beat until light and creamy. Add the egg and beat until fully incorporated.

3 In a separate bowl, sift the flour with the bicarbonate of soda and salt.

4 Fold half of the flour mixture into the butter mixture. Mix in the milk and buttermilk, then add the rest of the flour mixture and mix until fully incorporated. Transfer half of the cake mixture (batter) into another bowl and fold the sifted cocoa powder into this cake mixture until fully incorporated.

5 Using a piping (pastry) bag fitted with a large plain nozzle, pipe 24 3cm/1¼in rounds of vanilla cake mixture 4cm/½in apart on each of the baking trays. Place a dollop of the chocolate cake mixture in the centre of each piped vanilla round and, using the tip of a knife, swirl the cake mixture to create a marbled effect.

6 Bake for 10–12 minutes, or until the cakes bounce back when gently pressed. Transfer to a wire rack and leave to cool completely.

7 For the filling, place the icing sugar, vanilla seeds and butter in a bowl. Using an electric whisk on medium speed, whisk until crumbly. Slowly whisk in the cream, then increase the speed to high and whisk until smooth. Fold in the cocoa powder.

8 Place a tablespoonful of filling on to the flat side of one cake and top with the flat side of another. Repeat to make 24 pies. Spread melted chocolate over the top of each pie.

Nutritional information: Energy 270kcal/1139kJ; Protein 3g; Carbohydrate 35g, of which sugars 24g; Fat 15g, of which saturates 9g; Cholesterol 42mg; Calcium 38mg; Fibre 0.5g; Sodium 113mg.

Carrot cake whoopie pies

The sweetness of grated carrots adds a lovely moist touch to these whoopie pies. Delicately flavoured with cinnamon, nutmeg and orange rind, with crunch from the walnuts and a light cream cheese filling, these are a wonderful take on the traditional carrot cake.

MAKES 12 WHOOPIE PIES

For the cakes
150g/5oz/10 tbsp unsalted
  butter, softened
150g/5oz/generous ½ cup soft light
  brown sugar
seeds of 1 vanilla pod (bean)
2 eggs
300g/11oz/2¾ cups plain
  (all-purpose) flour
7.5ml/1½ tsp bicarbonate of soda
  (baking soda)
5ml/1 tsp salt
2.5ml/½ tsp freshly grated nutmeg
5ml/1 tsp ground cinnamon
100ml/3½fl oz/scant ½ cup buttermilk
175g/6oz carrots, finely grated and
  excess juice squeezed out
75g/3oz/¾ cup walnuts,
  roughly chopped

For the cream cheese filling
120ml/4fl oz/½ cup double
  (heavy) cream
100g/3¾oz/scant ½ cup cream cheese
15ml/1 tbsp clear honey
finely grated rind and juice of
  ½ small orange

For the icing
165g/5½oz/scant 1½ cups icing
  (confectioners') sugar
30ml/2 tbsp orange juice

1 Preheat the oven to 180°C/350°F/ Gas 4. Line two baking trays with baking parchment or silicone mats.

2 To make the cakes, whisk together the butter, brown sugar and vanilla seeds in a bowl until light and fluffy. Whisk in the eggs, one at a time.

3 In a separate bowl, sift the flour with the bicarbonate of soda, salt, nutmeg and cinnamon. Fold half of the dry ingredients into the butter mixture. Mix in the buttermilk, then add the remainder of the dry ingredients and mix until fully incorporated. Fold in the carrots and walnuts.

4 Using a piping (pastry) bag fitted with a large plain nozzle, pipe 12 5cm/ 2in rounds of cake mixture (batter) 5cm/2in apart on each baking tray. Bake for 12–15 minutes, or until the cakes bounce back when gently pressed. Transfer to a wire rack to cool.

5 For the filling, whip the cream in a bowl until medium-firm peaks form, then whisk in the cream cheese, honey and orange rind and juice until fully incorporated and stiff peaks form.

6 For the icing, mix the icing sugar and orange juice together in a small bowl to form a smooth, thick paste. Using a piping bag fitted with a star-shaped nozzle, pipe some filling on to the flat side of one cake and top with the flat side of another. Repeat to make 12 pies. Spread a little icing over the top of each pie to serve.

Nutritional information: Energy 432kcal/1812kJ; Protein 5g; Carbohydrate 49g, of which sugars 30g; Fat 25g, of which saturates 13g; Cholesterol 89mg; Calcium 86mg; Fibre 1.7g; Sodium 195mg.

White vanilla whoopie pies

Sandwiched together with a cream cheese filling and covered in melted white chocolate, these whoopie pies combine a light filling with deep and rich vanilla-flavoured cakes. Try adding a little raspberry jam in the middle with the filling for a splash of colour.

MAKES 12 WHOOPIE PIES

For the cakes
130g/4½oz/generous ½ cup unsalted
   butter, softened
150g/5oz/¾ cup caster
   (superfine) sugar
seeds of 2 vanilla pods (beans)
1 egg
325g/11½oz/scant 3 cups plain
   (all-purpose) flour
7.5ml/1½ tsp bicarbonate of soda
   (baking soda)
5ml/1 tsp salt
50ml/2fl oz/¼ cup milk
150ml/¼ pint/⅔ cup buttermilk

For the cream cheese filling
100ml/3½fl oz/scant ½ cup double
   (heavy) cream
150g/5oz/⅔ cup cream cheese
40g/1½oz/3 tbsp caster
   (superfine) sugar
seeds of 1 vanilla pod (bean)

For the topping
150g/5oz white chocolate, melted

1 Preheat the oven to 180°C/350°F/ Gas 4. Line two baking trays with baking parchment or silicone mats.

2 To make the cakes, whisk the butter, sugar and vanilla seeds in a bowl until light and fluffy. Whisk in the egg.

3 In a separate bowl, sift the flour with the bicarbonate of soda and salt. Fold half of the dry ingredients into the butter mixture. Mix in the milk and buttermilk, then mix in the rest of the dry ingredients.

4 Using a piping (pastry) bag fitted with a large plain nozzle, pipe 12 5cm/ 2in rounds of cake mixture (batter) 5cm/2in apart on each baking tray. Bake for 12–15 minutes, or until the cakes bounce back when pressed. Transfer to a wire rack to cool.

5 For the filling, whip the cream until firm peaks form, then whisk in the cream cheese, sugar and vanilla seeds.

6 To assemble the pies, using a piping bag fitted with a star-shaped nozzle, pipe a thick round of cream cheese filling on to the flat side of one cake and top with the flat side of another cake. Repeat with the remaining cakes and cream cheese filling to make 12 pies. Spread a little melted chocolate over the top of each pie. Allow the chocolate to set before serving.

Nutritional information: Energy 512kcal/2152kJ; Protein 9g; Carbohydrate 67g, of which sugars 26g; Fat 25g, of which saturates 15g; Cholesterol 87mg; Calcium 155mg; Fibre 2.0g; Sodium 380mg.

Gluten-free whoopie pies

Dark and rich, these gluten-free chocolate whoopie pie cakes are delicious on their own, straight out of the oven, or equally yummy served cold, sandwiched together with chocolate buttercream. Adding xanthan gum to the cake batter will give a softer texture to the cakes.

2 For the cakes, whisk the butter, sugar and vanilla seeds until light and fluffy. Whisk in the eggs.

3 In a separate bowl, sift the flour with the cocoa powder, xanthan gum, bicarbonate of soda and salt. Fold half of the dry ingredients into the butter mixture. Mix in the buttermilk and milk, then add the remainder of the dry ingredients and mix until fully incorporated.

MAKES 12 WHOOPIE PIES

140g/4¾oz unsalted butter, softened
165g/5½oz soft light brown sugar
seeds of 1 vanilla pod (bean)
2 eggs
200g/7oz gluten-free flour (see Cook's Tip)
50g/2oz unsweetened cocoa powder
7.5ml/1½ tsp xanthan gum (see Cook's Tip)
5ml/1 tsp bicarbonate of soda (baking soda)
5ml/1 tsp salt
275ml/8½fl oz/generous 1 cup buttermilk
175ml/6fl oz/¾ cup milk

For the filling
200ml/7fl oz/scant 1 cup double (heavy) cream
45ml/3 tbsp caster (superfine) sugar
25g/1oz unsweetened cocoa powder

1 Preheat the oven to 180°C/350°F/ Gas 4. Line two baking trays with baking parchment or silicone mats.

COOK'S TIP
You could use self-raising (self-rising) gluten-free flour, which is a blend of different flours, with added xanthan gum. If using this, leave out the bicarbonate of soda and xanthan gum in this recipe.

4 Using a piping (pastry) bag fitted with a large plain nozzle, pipe 12 5cm/2in rounds of cake mixture (batter) 5cm/2in apart on each baking tray. Bake for 12–15 minutes, or until the cakes bounce back when pressed. Transfer to a wire rack to cool.

5 For the filling, whisk the cream and sugar in a bowl with an electric whisk on high until just stiff. Gently fold in the sifted cocoa powder.

6 To assemble the pies, using a piping bag fitted with a star-shaped nozzle, pipe some filling on to the flat side of one cake and top with the flat side of another. Repeat to make 12 pies.

Nutritional information: Energy 326kcal/1387kJ; Protein 4g; Carbohydrate 34g, of which sugars 20g; Fat 21g, of which saturates 13g; Cholesterol 89mg; Calcium 62mg; Fibre 0.9g; Sodium 152mg.

Mini lemon drop whoopie pies

These lemon-flavoured whoopie pies are a cocktail-lover's delight with their citrus burst and zesty undertone. They create a perfect dinner party dessert thanks to their hint of limoncello, which gives them a truly scrumptious grown-up flavour.

MAKES 24 WHOOPIE PIES

For the cakes
125g/4¼oz/8½ tbsp unsalted butter, softened
175g/6oz/¾ cup soft light brown sugar
seeds of 1 vanilla pod (bean)
5ml/1 tsp lemon extract
1 egg
350g/12oz/3 cups plain (all-purpose) flour
7.5ml/1½ tsp bicarbonate of soda (baking soda)
5ml/1 tsp salt
250ml/8fl oz/1 cup buttermilk

For the ganache filling
150g/5oz white chocolate, chopped
65g/2½oz/5 tbsp unsalted butter, softened
100ml/3½fl oz/scant ½ cup double (heavy) cream
30ml/2 tbsp limoncello

For the lemon glaze
90ml/6 tbsp icing (confectioners') sugar
finely grated rind and juice of 1 large lemon

1 Preheat the oven to 180°C/350°F/ Gas 4. Line two baking trays with baking parchment or silicone mats.

2 To make the cakes, whisk the butter, brown sugar, vanilla seeds and lemon extract in a bowl until light and fluffy. Whisk in the egg.

3 In a separate bowl, sift the flour with the bicarbonate of soda and salt.

4 Fold half of the dry ingredients into the butter mixture. Mix in the buttermilk, then mix in the remainder of the dry ingredients.

5 Using a piping (pastry) bag fitted with a large plain nozzle, pipe 24 3cm/ 1¼in rounds of cake mixture (batter) 4cm/1½in apart on each baking tray. Bake for 10–12 minutes, or until the cakes bounce back when pressed. Transfer to a wire rack to cool.

6 To make the filling, place the white chocolate and butter in a heatproof bowl. Heat the double cream in a pan to the point just before it boils, then pour it over the butter and chocolate, and stir until smooth. Stir in the limoncello. Cover with clear film (plastic wrap) and refrigerate for 30 minutes–1 hour, until thickened.

7 To make the glaze, mix the icing sugar and lemon rind and juice in a small bowl, forming a smooth paste.

8 To assemble the pies, place a tablespoonful of ganache on to the flat side of one cake, then sandwich together with the flat side of another. Repeat with the remaining cakes and ganache to make 24 pies. Brush the lemon glaze over the tops of the pies and serve immediately.

Nutritional information: Energy 215kcal/904kJ; Protein 3g; Carbohydrate 27g, of which sugars 16g; Fat 11g, of which saturates 7g; Cholesterol 34mg; Calcium 59mg; Fibre 0.5g; Sodium 172mg.

Caffè latte whoopie pies

For a perfect afternoon pick-me-up, these whoopie pies hit the spot with their spicy flavour, light coffee cream and mocha topping. They look attractive decorated with chocolate-coated coffee beans and drizzled with chocolate.

MAKES 12 WHOOPIE PIES

For the cakes
125g/4¼oz/8½ tbsp unsalted
   butter, softened
175g/6oz/¾ cup soft light
   brown sugar
seeds of 1 vanilla pod (bean)
1 egg
350g/12oz/3 cups plain
   (all-purpose) flour
7.5ml/1½ tsp bicarbonate of soda
   (baking soda)
5ml/1 tsp salt
5ml/1 tsp freshly grated nutmeg
5ml/1 tsp ground cinnamon
250ml/8fl oz/1 cup buttermilk
45ml/3 tbsp instant coffee granules
   or powder, dissolved in 15ml/
   1 tbsp hot water

For the filling and topping
30ml/2 tbsp instant coffee granules
   or powder
250ml/8fl oz/1 cup whipping cream
100g/3¾oz coffee-flavoured
   chocolate, melted
36 chocolate-covered coffee beans

1 Preheat the oven to 180°C/350°F/
Gas 4. Line two baking trays with baking parchment or silicone mats. For the cakes, whisk the butter in a bowl with the sugar and vanilla seeds until light and fluffy. Whisk in the egg.

2 In a separate bowl, sift the flour with the bicarbonate of soda, salt and spices. Fold half of the dry ingredients into the butter mixture, then mix in the buttermilk.

3 Incorporate the remaining dry ingredients, then stir in the dissolved coffee. Using a piping (pastry) bag fitted with a large plain nozzle, pipe 12 5cm/2in rounds of cake mixture (batter) 5cm/2in apart on each baking tray. Bake for 12–15 minutes, or until the cakes bounce back when pressed. Transfer to a wire rack to cool.

4 For the filling, stir the coffee into a little of the cream, then add to the rest of the cream and whip until stiff.

5 Using a piping bag fitted with a star-shaped nozzle, pipe some filling on to the flat side of one cake and cover with the flat side of another. Repeat to make 12 pies. Pipe a 'nest' of the remaining filling on top of each pie. Top with 3 coffee beans, then drizzle melted chocolate over the top.

Nutritional information: Energy 380kcal/1597kJ; Protein 6g; Carbohydrate 45g, of which sugars 23g; Fat 21g, of which saturates 13g; Cholesterol 68mg; Calcium 117mg; Fibre 1.1g; Sodium 341mg.

Mocha whoopie pies

For caffeine lovers, these whoopie pies deliver a real coffee kick. Topped and filled with a light and sweet buttercream filling, they are best served with a tall glass of cold milk. Some of the luxurious filling is reserved for the top, so they look beautifully elegant.

MAKES 12 WHOOPIE PIES

For the cakes
130g/4½oz/generous ½ cup unsalted butter, softened
150g/5oz/¾ cup caster (superfine) sugar
seeds of 1 vanilla pod (bean)
1 egg
325g/11½oz/scant 3 cups plain (all-purpose) flour
7.5ml/1½ tsp bicarbonate of soda (baking soda)
5ml/1 tsp salt
150ml/¼ pint/⅔ cup buttermilk
50ml/2fl oz/¼ cup milk
60ml/4 tbsp instant coffee granules or powder dissolved in 15ml/ 1 tbsp hot water

For the filling and topping
30ml/2 tbsp instant coffee granules or powder, dissolved in 7.5ml/ 1½ tsp hot water
2 egg whites
125g/4½oz/generous ½ cup caster (superfine) sugar
225g/8oz/1 cup unsalted butter, softened
40g/1½oz dark (bittersweet) chocolate

1 Preheat the oven to 180°C/350°F/ Gas 4. Line two baking trays with baking parchment or silicone mats.

2 For the cakes, whisk the butter, sugar and vanilla seeds together until light and fluffy. Whisk in the egg. In a separate bowl, sift the flour with the bicarbonate of soda and salt. In a measuring jug (cup), mix the buttermilk, milk and dissolved coffee.

3 Fold half of the dry ingredients into the butter mixture. Mix in the buttermilk mixture, then add the remainder of the dry ingredients and mix well. Using a piping (pastry) bag fitted with a large plain nozzle, pipe 12 5cm/2in rounds of cake mixture (batter) 5cm/2in apart on each baking tray. Bake for 12–15 minutes, or until the cakes bounce back when pressed. Transfer to a wire rack to cool.

4 For the filling, put the egg whites and sugar in a heatproof bowl set over a pan of simmering water. Using an electric whisk, whisk until the sugar has dissolved and the mixture turns white and is hot. Remove from the heat and continue to whisk on high speed until the bowl starts to cool down. Turn the speed to low and whisk in the butter, a little at a time. Gently fold in the dissolved coffee.

5 Using a piping (pastry) bag fitted with a star-shaped nozzle, pipe some of the filling on to the flat side of one cake and top with the flat side of another. Repeat to make 12 pies. Pipe the remaining filling on the tops of the pies, then grate chocolate over the top.

COOK'S TIP
Experiment with different graters for various chocolate shavings.

Nutritional information: Energy 439kcal/1850kJ; Protein 5g; Carbohydrate 48g, of which sugars 27g; Fat 26g, of which saturates 17g; Cholesterol 88mg; Calcium 73mg; Fibre 1.0g; Sodium 335mg.

Mint and chocolate mini whoopie pies

The classic combination of mint and chocolate works beautifully in these decadent whoopie pies, perfect as a substitute for more conventional after-dinner mints. For a stronger minty flavour, finely chop some dark mint chocolates and add to the buttercream filling.

MAKES 24 WHOOPIE PIES

For the cakes
125g/4¼oz/8½ tbsp unsalted
  butter, softened
175g/6oz/¾ cup soft light
  brown sugar
seeds of 1 vanilla pod (bean)
1 egg
300g/11oz/2¾ cups plain
  (all-purpose) flour
40g/1½oz unsweetened cocoa powder
7.5ml/1½ tsp bicarbonate of soda
  (baking soda)
5ml/1 tsp salt
250ml/8fl oz/1 cup buttermilk

For the filling
2 egg whites
125g/4¼oz/generous ½ cup caster
  (superfine) sugar
225g/8oz/1 cup unsalted
  butter, softened
40g/1½oz unsweetened cocoa powder
4–5 drops peppermint extract

For the topping
100g/3¾oz dark (bittersweet)
  chocolate, melted
24 fresh mint leaves

1 Preheat the oven to 180°C/350°F/ Gas 4. Line two baking trays with baking parchment or silicone mats.

2 To make the cakes, whisk the butter, sugar and vanilla seeds together until light and creamy. Whisk in the egg.

3 In a separate bowl, sift the flour with the cocoa powder, bicarbonate of soda and salt.

4 Fold half of the dry ingredients into the butter mixture. Mix in the buttermilk, then add the remainder of the dry ingredients and mix until fully incorporated.

5 Using a piping (pastry) bag fitted with a large plain nozzle, pipe 24 3cm/1¼in rounds of cake mixture (batter) 4cm/1½in apart on each baking tray. Bake for 10–12 minutes, or until the cakes bounce back when gently pressed. Transfer to a wire rack to cool.

6 To make the filling, put the egg whites and sugar in a heatproof bowl and place the bowl over a pan of gently simmering water. Using an electric whisk, whisk the ingredients together until the sugar has dissolved and the mixture is white and hot.

7 Remove the bowl from the heat and continue to whisk the mixture on high speed until the bottom of the bowl starts to cool down. Turn the speed down to low and whisk in the butter, about 15g/½oz/1 tbsp at a time, making sure that each addition is fully incorporated before adding the next. Gently fold in the sifted cocoa powder and peppermint extract until fully incorporated.

8 To assemble the pies, place a tablespoon of filling on to the flat side of one cake and top with the flat side of another. Repeat with the remaining cakes and filling to make 24 pies. When you are ready to serve them, spread a little melted chocolate over the tops, and place a mint leaf on each one. If done in advance, the mint leaves will start to wilt.

Nutritional information: Energy 238kcal/1001kJ; Protein 3g; Carbohydrate 26g, of which sugars 16g; Fat 14g, of which saturates 9g; Cholesterol 44mg; Calcium 44mg; Fibre 0.5g; Sodium 196mg.

Fruity and nutty whoopies

Fresh and flavourful, many of the recipes in this chapter are perfect for a quick afternoon pick-me-up or lunchbox treat. For breakfast or a mid-morning snack, try the Banana Bread Whoopie Pies or the Oatmeal and Raisin Breakfast Whoopie Pies, or for something a little different, try the sumptuous Orange Polenta Whoopie Pies. For a healthier version, add extra chopped fruit, fill with yogurt instead of cream and sprinkle with extra chopped nuts. You can vary fruits according to season or personal taste.

Banana bread whoopie pies

Comforting and sweet, the cakes from these whoopies are excellent served while still warm, straight from the oven, smeared with the walnut buttercream or simply with chocolate spread or jam. They are moist and luxurious with a hint of cinnamon, and can also be toasted just before assembling.

2 For the cakes, cream the butter, sugar and vanilla seeds until light and fluffy. Beat in the eggs, one at a time. In a separate bowl, sift the flour with the bicarbonate of soda, cinnamon and salt. Fold half of the dry ingredients into the butter mixture. Mix in the buttermilk, then the remainder of the dry ingredients. Fold in the bananas.

3 Using a piping (pastry) bag fitted with a large plain nozzle, pipe 12 5cm/2in rounds of cake mixture (batter) 5cm/2in apart on each baking tray. Bake for 12–15 minutes, or until the cakes bounce back when gently pressed. Transfer to a wire rack to cool.

4 For the filling, place the icing sugar, vanilla seeds and butter in a bowl. Using an electric whisk on medium speed, whisk until crumbly. Slowly whisk in the cream, then increase the speed to high and whisk until smooth. Fold in the walnuts.

MAKES 12 WHOOPIE PIES

For the cakes
150g/5oz/10 tbsp unsalted
  butter, softened
150g/5oz/generous ½ cup soft light
  brown sugar
seeds of 1 vanilla pod (bean)
2 eggs
325g/11½oz/scant 3 cups plain
  (all-purpose) flour
7.5ml/1½ tsp bicarbonate of soda
  (baking soda)
5ml/1 tsp ground cinnamon
2.5ml/½ tsp salt
100ml/3½fl oz/scant ½ cup buttermilk
200g/7oz mashed bananas

For the buttercream filling
300g/11oz/2¾ cups icing
  (confectioners') sugar
seeds of 1 vanilla pod (bean)
150g/5oz/10 tbsp unsalted
  butter, softened
50ml/2fl oz/¼ cup double
  (heavy) cream
75g/3oz/¾ cup walnuts,
  finely chopped

icing (confectioners') sugar,
  for dusting

1 Preheat the oven to 180°C/350°F/ Gas 4. Line two baking trays with baking parchment or silicone mats.

5 Using a piping bag fitted with a large plain nozzle, pipe small blobs of the filling on to the flat side of one cake, then top with the flat side of another. Repeat to make 12 pies. Dust with icing sugar, using a doily to create a pattern.

Nutritional information: Energy 520kcal/2191kJ; Protein 5g; Carbohydrate 64g, of which sugars 43g; Fat 29g, of which saturates 16g; Cholesterol 102mg; Calcium 77mg; Fibre 1.9g; Sodium 250mg.

Oatmeal and raisin breakfast whoopie pies

These hearty whoopie pies, filled with juicy raisins and wholesome oats, are a perfect mid-morning treat. They are flavoured with a hint of cinnamon and sandwiched together with a creamy cheese filling, and go well with a cup of tea or coffee.

MAKES 12 WHOOPIE PIES

For the cakes
130g/4½oz/generous ½ cup unsalted
   butter, softened
150g/5oz/¾ cup caster
   (superfine) sugar
seeds of 1 vanilla pod (bean)
1 egg
325g/11½oz/scant 3 cups plain
   (all-purpose) flour
7.5ml/1½ tsp bicarbonate of soda
   (baking soda)
5ml/1 tsp ground cinnamon
5ml/1 tsp salt
150ml/¼ pint/⅔ cup buttermilk
50ml/2fl oz/¼ cup milk
40g/1½oz/scant ½ cup rolled oats
100g/3¾oz/⅔ cup raisins

For the mascarpone filling
120ml/4fl oz/½ cup double
   (heavy) cream
125g/4½oz/generous ½ cup
   mascarpone
25ml/1½ tbsp caster (superfine) sugar
seeds from 1 vanilla pod (bean)

1 Preheat the oven to 180°C/350°F/ Gas 4. Line two baking trays with baking parchment or silicone mats.

2 To make the cakes, whisk the butter, sugar and vanilla seeds in a bowl until light and fluffy. Whisk in the egg.

3 In a separate bowl, sift the flour with the bicarbonate of soda, cinnamon and salt. Fold half of the dry ingredients into the butter mixture. Add the buttermilk and milk, and mix well.

4 Mix in the remaining dry ingredients, then stir in the oats and raisins. Using a piping (pastry) bag fitted with a large plain nozzle, pipe 12 5cm/2in rounds of cake mixture (batter) 5cm/2in apart on each baking tray. Bake for 12–15 minutes, or until the cakes bounce back when pressed. Transfer to a wire rack to cool.

5 For the filling, whip the cream until medium-firm peaks form, then whisk in the mascarpone, sugar and vanilla seeds until stiff peaks form. Using a piping bag fitted with a small star-shaped nozzle, pipe some filling on to the flat side of one cake and top with the flat side of another. Repeat to make 12 pies.

Nutritional information: Energy 366kcal/1537kJ; Protein 5g; Carbohydrate 44g, of which sugars 21g; Fat 20g, of which saturates 13g; Cholesterol 70mg; Calcium 88mg; Fibre 1.7g; Sodium 334mg.

Orange polenta whoopie pies

These dense and substantial whoopie pies combine the zesty flavours of orange and chocolate in a delicious creamy filling that sandwiches together soft polenta cakes. You can try experimenting with the rind and juice of other citrus fruits, such as mandarins or limes.

MAKES 12 WHOOPIE PIES

For the cakes
175g/6oz/1½ cups instant polenta
juice of 1 orange
125g/4¼oz/8½ tbsp unsalted
  butter, softened
200g/7oz/scant 1 cup soft light
  brown sugar
2 eggs
450g/1lb/4 cups plain (all-purpose)
  flour
7.5ml/1½ tsp bicarbonate of soda
  (baking soda)
5ml/1 tsp salt
250ml/8fl oz/1 cup buttermilk

For the filling
250ml/8fl oz/1 cup double
  (heavy) cream
25g/1oz/2 tbsp caster
  (superfine) sugar
grated rind and juice of ½ orange
20g/¾oz unsweetened cocoa powder

For the topping
100g/3¾oz milk chocolate, melted

1 Preheat the oven to 180°C/350°F/ Gas 4. Line two baking trays with baking parchment or silicone mats. Place the polenta in a bowl and stir in the orange juice. Set aside to soak.

2 To make the cakes, place the butter and brown sugar in a bowl and whisk together until light and creamy. Whisk in the eggs, one at a time.

3 In a separate bowl, sift the flour with the bicarbonate of soda and salt. Add the dry ingredients to the butter mixture in three batches, alternating with the buttermilk. Fold in the polenta.

4 Using a piping (pastry) bag fitted with a large plain nozzle, pipe 12 5cm/2in rounds of cake mixture (batter) about 5cm/2in apart on each baking tray. Bake for 12–15 minutes, or until the cakes bounce back when gently pressed. Transfer to a wire rack to cool.

5 To make the filling, whip the cream until stiff peaks form. Add the sugar, orange rind and juice and cocoa powder, and whisk until thick.

6 Using a piping bag fitted with a star-shaped nozzle, pipe some of the filling on to the flat side of one cake and top with the flat side of another. Repeat to make 12 pies. Place the pies on a wire cooling rack and drizzle over the melted chocolate.

Nutritional information: Energy 432kcal/1815kJ; Protein 7g; Carbohydrate 57g, of which sugars 23g; Fat 21g, of which saturates 13g; Cholesterol 79mg; Calcium 95mg; Fibre 1.7g; Sodium 305mg.

Poppy seed whoopie pies

For a fresh taste of summer, these whoopie pies really hit the spot. With their poppy seed-flecked tops, they combine crunch and texture with a light and zesty buttercream filling. The orange flower water helps bring out the flavour of the orange rind in the cakes.

MAKES 12 WHOOPIE PIES

For the cakes
130g/4½oz/generous ½ cup unsalted butter, softened
150g/5oz/generous ½ cup soft light brown sugar
seeds of 1 vanilla pod (bean)
1 egg
300g/11oz/2¾ cups plain (all-purpose) flour
7.5ml/1½ tsp bicarbonate of soda (baking soda)
5ml/1 tsp salt
150ml/¼ pint/⅔ cup buttermilk
50ml/2fl oz/¼ cup milk
100g/3¾oz poppy seeds, plus extra to decorate
5ml/1 tsp orange flower water
finely grated rind of 1 orange

For the filling
2 egg whites
125g/4½oz/generous ½ cup caster (superfine) sugar
225g/8oz/1 cup unsalted butter, softened
finely grated rind of 1 orange
juice of ½ orange

For the icing
150g/5oz/1¼ cups icing (confectioners') sugar
25ml/1½ tbsp orange juice

1 Preheat the oven to 180°C/350°F/ Gas 4. Line two baking trays with baking parchment or silicone mats.

2 For the cakes, whisk the butter, sugar and vanilla seeds until light and fluffy. Whisk in the egg.

3 In a separate bowl, sift the flour with the bicarbonate of soda and salt. Fold half of the dry ingredients into the butter mixture. Mix in the buttermilk and milk, then the remainder of the dry ingredients. Mix in the poppy seeds, orange flower water and rind.

4 Using a piping (pastry) bag fitted with a large plain nozzle, pipe 12 5cm/ 2in rounds of cake mixture (batter) about 5cm/2in apart on each baking tray. Bake for 12–15 minutes, or until the cakes bounce back when pressed. Transfer to a wire rack to cool.

5 For the filling, put the egg whites and sugar in a heatproof bowl over a pan of simmering water. Whisk, with an electric whisk, until the sugar dissolves and the mixture is white and hot.

6 Remove from the heat and continue to whisk on high until the bowl starts to cool. Turn the speed to low and whisk in the butter, a little at a time. Fold in the orange rind and juice. For the icing, mix the icing sugar and juice. Using a star-shaped nozzle, pipe filling on to the flat side of one cake and top with the flat side of another. Repeat to make 12 pies. Spread icing on each pie and decorate with poppy seeds.

Nutritional information: Energy 458kcal/1934kJ; Protein 54; Carbohydrate 58g, of which sugars 38g; Fat 25g, of which saturates 16g; Cholesterol 88mg; Calcium 71mg; Fibre 0.9g; Sodium 327mg.

Orange blossom whoopie pies

A delightful, zesty and citrusy whoopie pie, with a light and fragrant honey buttercream filling. These whoopie pies can be made a few days in advance to allow all the flavours to completely infuse. Store them, wrapped in clear film (plastic wrap), in the refrigerator for up to 3 days.

1 Preheat the oven to 180°C/350°F/ Gas 4. Line two baking trays with baking parchment or silicone mats. For the cakes, whisk the butter, sugar and vanilla seeds in a bowl until light and fluffy. Whisk in the egg.

2 In a separate bowl, sift the flour with the bicarbonate of soda and salt. Stir in the orange rind. In a measuring jug (cup), mix the buttermilk, milk and orange flower water. Fold half of the dry ingredients into the butter mixture. Mix in the buttermilk mixture, then stir in the remainder of the dry ingredients.

3 Using a piping (pastry) bag fitted with a large plain nozzle, pipe 12 5cm/ 2in rounds of cake mixture (batter) about 5cm/2in apart on each baking tray. Bake for 12–15 minutes, or until the cakes bounce back when pressed. Transfer to a wire rack to cool.

MAKES 12 WHOOPIE PIES

For the cakes
130g/4½oz/generous ½ cup
  unsalted butter, softened
150g/5oz/¾ cup caster
  (superfine) sugar
seeds of 1 vanilla pod (bean)
1 egg
325g/11½oz/scant 3 cups plain
  (all-purpose) flour
7.5ml/1½ tsp bicarbonate of soda
  (baking soda)
5ml/1 tsp salt
finely grated rind of 1 orange
150ml/¼ pint/⅔ cup buttermilk
50ml/2fl oz/¼ cup milk
10ml/2 tsp orange flower water

For the filling
2 egg whites
125g/4¼oz/generous ½ cup caster
  (superfine) sugar
225g/8oz/1 cup unsalted butter,
  softened
finely grated rind and juice of
  ½ orange
5ml/1 tsp orange flower water
15ml/1 tbsp clear honey

For the icing and decoration
150g/5oz/1¼ cups icing
  (confectioners') sugar
25ml/1½ tbsp orange juice
finely grated orange rind and
  orange-flavoured mini sweets
  (candies), to decorate

4 For the filling, put the egg whites and sugar in a heatproof bowl over a pan of simmering water. Using an electric whisk, whisk until the sugar has dissolved and the mixture is white and hot. Remove from the heat and whisk on high until the bowl starts to cool. Turn the speed to low and whisk in the butter, a little at a time. Fold in the rind and juice, orange flower water and honey.

5 Mix the icing sugar and juice to form a smooth paste. Using a star-shaped nozzle, pipe filling on to the flat side of one cake and top with the flat side of another. Repeat to make 12 pies. Top each with icing, rind and sweets.

Nutritional information: Energy 486kcal/2052kJ; Protein 4g; Carbohydrate 63g, of which sugars 42g; Fat 26g, of which saturates 16g; Cholesterol 88mg; Calcium 69mg; Fibre 1.0g; Sodium 335mg.

Lemon curd whoopie pies

The lemon curd filling used here delivers a tart punch, which, when combined with the sweet cakes, creates a fresh and zesty teatime treat. Any leftover lemon curd can be stored in an airtight container in the refrigerator for 3 weeks. You could use store-bought lemon curd instead.

MAKES 12 WHOOPIE PIES

For the cakes
125g/4¼oz/8½ tbsp unsalted butter, softened
175g/6oz/¾ cup soft light brown sugar
seeds of 1 vanilla pod (bean)
1 egg
300g/11oz/2¾ cup plain (all-purpose) flour
7.5ml/1½ tsp bicarbonate of soda (baking soda)
5ml/1 tsp salt
250ml/8fl oz/1 cup buttermilk
finely grated rind of 1 lemon
5ml/1 tsp lemon extract

For the lemon curd filling
3 eggs, lightly beaten
finely grated rind and juice of 3 lemons
200g/7oz/1 cup caster (superfine) sugar
100g/3¾oz/scant ½ cup unsalted butter, diced

For the icing and decoration
150g/5oz/1¼ cups icing (confectioners') sugar
juice of 1 lemon
pared lemon rind and sprinkles

1 Preheat the oven to 180°C/350°F/Gas 4. Line two baking trays with baking parchment or silicone mats.

2 To make the cakes, place the butter, brown sugar and vanilla seeds in a bowl and whisk together until light and creamy. Add the egg and whisk until fully incorporated.

3 In a separate bowl, sift the flour with the bicarbonate of soda and salt. In a measuring jug (cup), mix the buttermilk, lemon rind and lemon extract together. Fold half of the dry ingredients into the butter mixture. Mix in the buttermilk mixture, then the remainder of the dry ingredients.

4 Using a piping (pastry) bag fitted with a large plain nozzle, pipe 12 5cm/2in rounds of mixture (batter) about 5cm/2in apart on each baking tray.

5 Bake for 12–15 minutes, or until the cakes bounce back when pressed. Transfer to a wire rack to cool.

6 Put all the filling ingredients in a heatproof bowl set over a pan of simmering water. Stir over low heat for 10 minutes, or until the mixture thickens. Be careful not to allow the mixture to boil or overheat, otherwise it will curdle. Remove from the heat, leave to cool, then cover with clear film (plastic wrap) and refrigerate until required.

7 Mix the icing sugar and lemon juice to form a smooth, thick paste. Place a tablespoonful of lemon curd on to the flat side of one cake and top with the flat side of another. Repeat to make 12 pies. Spread a little icing over the top of each pie and decorate with lemon rind and sprinkles.

Nutritional information: Energy 431kcal/1824kJ; Protein 6g; Carbohydrate 66g, of which sugars 47g; Fat 18g, of which saturates 11g; Cholesterol 121mg; Calcium 86mg; Fibre 0.9g; Sodium 351mg.

Raspberry swirl whoopie pies

Pretty and pink, these raspberry swirl whoopies are eye-catching and can be made at any time of the year with frozen raspberries. They look attractive as they are, but if you want to make a topping, simply mash some raspberries with some icing (confectioners') sugar and drizzle on top.

MAKES 12 WHOOPIE PIES

For the cakes
125g/4¼oz/8½ tbsp unsalted
  butter, softened
175g/6oz/¾ cup soft light brown sugar
seeds of 1 vanilla pod (bean)
1 egg
350g/12oz/3 cups plain
  (all-purpose) flour
7.5ml/1½ tsp bicarbonate of soda
  (baking soda)
5ml/1 tsp salt
250ml/8fl oz/1 cup buttermilk
5ml/1 tsp red food colouring

For the filling
200ml/7fl oz/scant 1 cup
  whipping cream
150g/5oz/scant 1 cup fresh raspberries

1 Preheat the oven to 180°C/350°F/ Gas 4. Line two baking trays with baking parchment or silicone mats.

2 To make the cakes, place the butter, brown sugar and vanilla seeds in a bowl and whisk together until light and creamy. Add the egg and whisk until fully incorporated.

3 In a separate bowl, sift the flour with the bicarbonate of soda and salt. Fold half of the dry ingredients into the butter mixture. Mix in the buttermilk, then add the rest of the dry ingredients and mix until fully incorporated. Transfer half of the cake mixture (batter) into another bowl and fold the red food colouring into this cake mixture.

4 Using a piping (pastry) bag fitted with a large plain nozzle, pipe 12 3cm/1¼in rounds of vanilla cake mixture 5cm/2in apart on each baking tray. Place a dollop of the red mixture on each round and, using the tip of a knife, swirl a figure of eight to create a marbled effect.

5 Bake for 12–15 minutes, or until the cakes bounce back when pressed. Transfer to a wire rack to cool.

6 For the filling, whip the cream in a bowl until stiff peaks form. Squash the raspberries with the back of a fork, then fold them into the cream.

7 Place a tablespoonful of raspberry cream filling on to the flat side of one cake and top with the flat side of another. Repeat to make 12 pies.

Nutritional information: Energy 312kcal/1313kJ; Protein 5g; Carbohydrate 40g, of which sugars 17g; Fat 16g, of which saturates 10g; Cholesterol 61mg; Calcium 91mg; Fibre 1.9g; Sodium 331mg.

Pavlova raspberry crunch whoopie pies

This is a completely different whoopie pie and well worth the extra time it takes. The method uses an electric stand mixer to make the meringue, but if you do not have one, you can use an electric whisk and a mixing bowl, but you will need someone to pour in the hot sugar for you.

MAKES 12 WHOOPIE PIES

For the meringue cakes
250g/9oz/scant 1⅓ cups caster
    (superfine) sugar
4 egg whites

For the filling
250ml/8fl oz/1 cup whipping cream
40g/1½oz/3 tbsp caster
    (superfine) sugar
75g/3oz/½ cup fresh raspberries

icing (confectioners') sugar,
    to decorate

1 Preheat the oven to 150°C/300°F/ Gas 2. Line two baking trays with baking parchment or silicone mats.

2 To make the meringue cakes, spread the sugar out thinly on one of the baking trays and place in the oven for about 5 minutes, or until the sugar is hot, and just before it begins to melt.

3 Place the egg whites in the bowl of an electric stand mixer. Just before the sugar is ready to come out of the oven, start whisking them on high speed until stiff peaks form. Remove the sugar from the oven and carefully pour it (by lifting both sides of the baking parchment) into the whisking egg whites.

4 Keep whisking until you have a thick, glossy meringue. This will take about 10 minutes. Return the parchment to the baking tray and reduce the oven temperature to 110°C/225°F/Gas ¼.

5 Using an ice cream scoop, scoop 12 balls of meringue mixture, spacing them slightly apart, on to each of the lined baking trays. Bake for 2½ hours, or until the meringues are crisp and dry, but still white. Transfer to a wire rack to cool.

6 To make the filling, whip the cream in a bowl until stiff peaks form. Add the sugar and whisk to mix. Place the raspberries on a plate and squash them roughly with the back of a fork. Add the crushed raspberries to the whipped cream mixture and fold in gently.

7 Place a tablespoonful of raspberry cream filling on to the flat side of one meringue cake and top with the flat side of another meringue cake. Repeat with the remaining meringue cakes and raspberry cream to make 12 pies. Dust the pies with sifted icing sugar, then serve.

Nutritional information: Energy 180kcal/756kJ; Protein 1g; Carbohydrate 26g, of which sugars 26g; Fat 8g, of which saturates 5g; Cholesterol 22mg; Calcium 17mg; Fibre 0.4g; Sodium 27mg.

Mango passion whoopie pies

Exotic and enticing, these whoopie pies are filled with mango pieces and topped with a passion fruit glaze. Try other tropical fruits, such as papaya and star fruit (carambola). They are best served immediately, but if making them in advance, store in the refrigerator and glaze just before serving.

1 Preheat the oven to 180°C/350°F/ Gas 4. Line two baking trays with baking parchment or silicone mats. For the cakes, whisk the butter, sugar and vanilla seeds until fluffy. Whisk in the egg. In a separate bowl, sift the flour with the bicarbonate of soda and salt. Fold half of the dry ingredients into the butter mixture. Mix in the buttermilk and milk, then the remainder of the dry ingredients.

2 Using a piping (pastry) bag fitted with a large plain nozzle, pipe 12 5cm/ 2in rounds of mixture (batter) 5cm/2in apart on each baking tray. Bake for 12–15 minutes, or until the cakes bounce back when pressed. Transfer to a wire rack to cool. For the filling, put the cream, vanilla seeds and sugar in a bowl and whisk until stiff peaks form. Fold in the chopped mango.

3 To make the glaze, mix the icing sugar and passion fruit juice together until smooth and syrupy. Place a tablespoonful of the filling on to the flat side of one cake and top with the flat side of another. Repeat to make 12 pies. Spread a little glaze over the top of each pie, then decorate with passion fruit pulp.

MAKES 12 WHOOPIE PIES

For the cakes
130g/4½oz/generous ½ cup
  unsalted butter, softened
150g/5oz/¾ cup caster
  (superfine) sugar
seeds of 1 vanilla pod (bean)
1 egg
325g/11½oz/scant 3 cups plain
  (all-purpose) flour
7.5ml/1½ tsp bicarbonate of soda
  (baking soda)
5ml/1 tsp salt
150ml/¼ pint/⅔ cup buttermilk
50ml/2fl oz/¼ cup milk

For the filling
200ml/7fl oz/scant 1 cup double
  (heavy) cream
seeds of 1 vanilla pod (bean)
25g/1oz/2 tbsp caster
  (superfine) sugar
½ mango, peeled, stoned (pitted)
  and finely chopped

For the glaze
90ml/6 tbsp icing
  (confectioners') sugar
juice of 2 passion fruits

pulp of 3 passion fruits, including
  seeds, to decorate

Nutritional information: Energy 363kcal/1526kJ; Protein 4g; Carbohydrate 47g, of which sugars 26g; Fat 19g, of which saturates 12g; Cholesterol 98mg; Calcium 74mg; Fibre 1.2g; Sodium 325mg.

Mandarin cheesecake whoopie pies

These delicious whoopie pies resemble a fresh and fruity cheesecake bursting with citrusy mandarin pieces and accentuated with warming hints of cinnamon and nutmeg. You can experiment with different flavours by using other fruits when they are in season.

MAKES 12 WHOOPIE PIES

For the cakes
125g/4¼oz/8½ tbsp unsalted
  butter, softened
175g/6oz/¾ cup soft light
  brown sugar
seeds of 1 vanilla pod (bean)
1 egg
350g/12oz/3 cups plain
  (all-purpose) flour
7.5ml/1½ tsp bicarbonate of soda
  (baking soda)
5ml/1 tsp salt
2.5ml/½ tsp ground cinnamon
2.5ml/½ tsp freshly grated nutmeg
250ml/8fl oz/1 cup buttermilk
grated rind and juice of 1 mandarin
10ml/2 tsp orange flower water

For the mandarin cheese filling
120ml/4fl oz/½ cup double
  (heavy) cream
125g/4½oz/generous ½ cup
  cream cheese
1 mandarin, peeled, segmented
  and finely chopped
15ml/1 tbsp clear honey
1.5ml/¼ tsp freshly grated nutmeg

For the icing
300g/11oz/2¾ cups icing
  (confectioners') sugar
50ml/2fl oz/¼ cup orange juice
a few drops of orange food colouring

20g/¾oz white mini marshmallows,
  to decorate

1 Preheat the oven to 180°C/350°F/ Gas 4. Line two baking trays with baking parchment or silicone mats.

2 For the cakes, whisk the butter, sugar and vanilla seeds until light and fluffy. Whisk in the egg.

3 In a separate bowl, sift the flour with the bicarbonate of soda, salt, cinnamon and nutmeg. In a measuring jug (cup), mix the buttermilk, mandarin rind and juice, and orange flower water together. Fold half of the dry ingredients into the butter mixture. Mix in the buttermilk mixture, then the remainder of the dry ingredients.

4 Using a piping (pastry) bag fitted with a large plain nozzle, pipe 12 5cm/2in rounds of cake mixture (batter) 5cm/2in apart on each baking tray. Bake for 12–15 minutes, or until the cakes bounce back when pressed. Transfer to a wire rack to cool.

5 To make the filling, whip the cream until medium-firm peaks form, then whisk in the cream cheese until thick. Add the mandarin pieces, honey and nutmeg, and fold everything together.

6 For the icing, mix the icing sugar, orange juice and food colouring to form a smooth paste. Using a piping (pastry) bag fitted with a small star-shaped nozzle, pipe some filling on to the flat side of one cake and top with the flat side of another. Repeat to make 12 pies. Spread icing on top of each pie and top with marshmallows.

Nutritional information: Energy 448kcal/1888kJ; Protein 4g; Carbohydrate 69g, of which sugars 46g; Fat 20g, of which saturates 12g; Cholesterol 48mg; Calcium 96mg; Fibre 1.2g; Sodium 391mg.

Strawberry lime cheesecake whoopie pies

The classic flavours of strawberry cheesecake are always a delight, and they are even better in a whoopie pie. These whoopies are filled with a creamy ricotta cheese mixture containing chopped fresh strawberries, and are perfect for the summer when the berries are at their best.

MAKES 12 WHOOPIE PIES

For the cakes
125g/4¼oz/8½ tbsp unsalted
  butter, softened
175g/6oz/¾ cup soft light
  brown sugar
seeds of 1 vanilla pod (bean)
1 egg
350g/12oz/3 cups plain
  (all-purpose) flour
7.5ml/1½ tsp bicarbonate of soda
  (baking soda)
5ml/1 tsp salt
finely grated rind of 2 limes
250ml/8fl oz/1 cup buttermilk

For the strawberry cheese filling
100ml/3½fl oz/scant ½ cup double
  (heavy) cream
100g/3¾oz/scant ½ cup ricotta cheese
25g/1oz/2 tbsp caster (superfine) sugar
seeds of 1 vanilla pod (bean)
finely grated rind of 1 lime
75g/3oz/¾ cup fresh strawberries

For the topping
100g/3¾oz white chocolate, melted
red and pink sprinkles

1 Preheat the oven to 180°C/350°F/
Gas 4. Line two baking trays with
baking parchment or silicone mats.

2 For the cakes, whisk the butter,
sugar and vanilla seeds in a bowl until
light and fluffy. Whisk in the egg.

3 In a separate bowl, sift the flour with
the bicarbonate of soda and salt. Mix
in the lime rind. Fold half of the dry
ingredients into the butter mixture.
Mix in the buttermilk, then the
remainder of the dry ingredients.

4 Using a piping (pastry) bag fitted
with a large plain nozzle, pipe 12
5cm/2in rounds of cake mixture
(batter) 5cm/2in apart on each baking
tray. Bake for 12–15 minutes, or until
the cakes bounce back when pressed.
Transfer to a wire rack to cool.

5 To make the filling, whip the
cream until stiff peaks form, then
whisk in the ricotta cheese, sugar,
vanilla seeds and lime rind, mixing
well. Hull and chop the strawberries,
then fold them into the mixture.

6 Place a heaped tablespoonful of
filling on to the flat side of one cake
and top with the flat side of another.
Repeat to make 12 pies. Spread a little
melted chocolate over the top of each
pie, and decorate with sprinkles.

Nutritional information: Energy 356kcal/1501kJ; Protein 6g; Carbohydrate 47g, of which sugars 25g; Fat 18g, of which saturates 11g; Cholesterol 60mg; Calcium 128mg; Fibre 1.2g; Sodium 347mg.

Key lime whoopie pies

The traditional dessert key lime pie originated in the western Florida Keys and uses a specific lime, the key lime, that grows there. However, normal limes can be used instead, if you cannot get hold of them. Store any leftover lime curd in an airtight container in the refrigerator for up to 3 weeks.

MAKES 12 WHOOPIE PIES

For the cakes
125g/4¼oz/8½ tbsp unsalted
   butter, softened
175g/6oz/¾ cup soft light
   brown sugar
seeds of 1 vanilla pod (bean)
1 egg
350g/12oz/3 cups plain
   (all-purpose) flour
7.5ml/1½ tsp bicarbonate of soda
   (baking soda)
5ml/1 tsp salt
250ml/8fl oz/1 cup buttermilk

For the lime curd filling
grated rind and juice of 3 limes
3 eggs
200g/7oz/1 cup caster
   (superfine) sugar
100g/3¾oz/scant ½ cup unsalted
   butter, diced

For the topping
150g/5oz/1¼ cups icing
   (confectioners') sugar
juice of 2 limes
finely grated lime rind and
   green sprinkles

1 Preheat the oven to 180°C/350°F/ Gas 4. Line two baking trays with baking parchment or silicone mats.

2 For the cakes, whisk the butter, sugar and vanilla seeds until light and creamy. Whisk in the egg. In a separate bowl, sift the flour with the bicarbonate of soda and salt. Fold half of the dry ingredients into the butter mixture.

3 Mix in the buttermilk, then mix in the remainder of the dry ingredients.

4 Using a piping (pastry) bag fitted with a large plain nozzle, pipe 12 5cm/ 2in rounds of cake mixture (batter) 5cm/2in apart on each baking tray. Bake for 12–15 minutes, or until the cakes bounce back when pressed. Transfer to a wire rack to cool.

5 To make the filling, put all the ingredients in a heatproof bowl set over a pan of simmering water and stir together. Heat over medium heat, stirring constantly, for 10 minutes, or until the mixture thickens. Do not allow it to boil or overheat, otherwise it will curdle. Remove from the heat and leave to cool, then cover with clear film (plastic wrap) and chill until required.

6 For the icing, mix the icing sugar and lime juice together in a small bowl to form a smooth, thick paste. Place a tablespoonful of lime curd on to the flat side of one cake and top with the flat side of another. Repeat to make 12 pies. Spread a little icing over the top of each pie and decorate with grated lime rind and sprinkles.

Nutritional information: Energy 446kcal/1885kJ; Protein 6g; Carbohydrate 69g, of which sugars 47g; Fat 18g, of which saturates 11g; Cholesterol 121mg; Calcium 92mg; Fibre 1.1g; Sodium 351mg.

Chestnut whoopie pies

These tasty whoopie pies are made with a medley of grown-up flavours: fresh roasted chestnuts, chestnut purée and rich dark chocolate. They are deeply satisfying and incredibly moreish, a real treat for adult tastebuds.

2 In a separate bowl, sift the flour with the bicarbonate of soda and salt. Fold half of the dry ingredients into the butter mixture. Mix in the buttermilk and milk, then the remainder of the dry ingredients. Fold in the chestnuts.

3 Using a piping (pastry) bag fitted with a large plain nozzle, pipe 12 5cm/2in rounds of cake mixture (batter) 5cm/2in apart on each baking tray. Bake for 12–15 minutes, or until pale golden. Transfer to a wire rack to cool.

MAKES 12 WHOOPIE PIES

For the cakes
130g/4½oz/generous ½ cup
  unsalted butter, softened
150g/5oz/¾ cup caster
  (superfine) sugar
seeds of 1 vanilla pod (bean)
1 egg
325g/11½oz/scant 3 cups plain
  (all-purpose) flour
7.5ml/1½ tsp bicarbonate of soda
  (baking soda)
5ml/1 tsp salt
150ml/¼ pint/⅔ cup buttermilk
50ml/2fl oz/¼ cup milk
100g/3¾oz roasted chestnuts,
  peeled and roughly chopped

For the filling
200g/7oz/generous ¾ cup
  chestnut purée
150g/5oz/⅔ cup mascarpone
100g/3¾oz/scant 1 cup icing
  (confectioners') sugar
75g/3oz dark (bittersweet)
  chocolate, melted

unsweetened cocoa powder,
  for dusting

1 Preheat the oven to 180°C/350°F/Gas 4. Line two baking trays with baking parchment or silicone mats. For the cakes, whisk the butter, sugar and vanilla seeds until creamy. Whisk in the egg.

4 For the filling, whisk together the chestnut purée, mascarpone and icing sugar. Slowly add the melted chocolate, whisking until combined. Place a tablespoonful of the filling on to the flat side of one cake and top with the flat side of another. Repeat to make 12 pies. Dust with cocoa powder.

Nutritional information: Energy 395kcal/1667kJ; Protein 5g; Carbohydrate 57g, of which sugars 29g; Fat 18g, of which saturates 11g; Cholesterol 58mg; Calcium 88mg; Fibre 2.5g; Sodium 331mg.

Salted caramel and chestnut whoopie pies

The classic taste of salted caramel combines beautifully with earthy chestnuts in these delicious whoopie pies. The chestnuts in the cake mixture make a lovely textural contrast to the smooth dulce de leche, and the additional crunch of the salt makes these whoopies a real delight.

MAKES 12 WHOOPIE PIES

125g/4¼oz/8½ tbsp unsalted
  butter, softened
175g/6oz/¾ cup soft light
  brown sugar
seeds of 1 vanilla pod (bean)
1 egg
300g/11oz/2¾ cups plain
  (all-purpose) flour
7.5ml/1½ tsp bicarbonate of soda
  (baking soda)
5ml/1 tsp salt
250ml/8fl oz/1 cup buttermilk
100g/3¾oz/scant 1 cup roasted
  chestnuts (shelled), chopped
250g/9oz dulce de leche
10g/¼oz fleur de sel (see Cook's Tip)

1 Preheat the oven to 180°C/350°F/ Gas 4. Line two baking trays with baking parchment or silicone mats.

2 Place the butter, brown sugar and vanilla seeds in a bowl and whisk together until creamy. Add the egg and whisk until fully incorporated.

3 In a separate bowl, sift the flour with the bicarbonate of soda and salt. Fold half of the dry ingredients into the butter mixture. Mix in the buttermilk, then add the remainder of the dry ingredients and mix until fully incorporated. Fold in the chestnuts, mixing well.

4 Using a piping (pastry) bag fitted with a large plain nozzle, pipe 12 5cm/2in rounds of cake mixture (batter) 5cm/2in apart on each of the lined baking trays.

5 Bake for 12–15 minutes, or until pale golden. Remove from the oven, transfer to a wire rack and leave to cool completely before assembling.

6 To assemble the pies, place a tablespoonful of the dulce de leche on to the flat side of one cake, sprinkle with a little fleur de sel and top with the flat side of another. Repeat to make 12 pies.

7 Spread each top with a teaspoonful of dulce de leche and sprinkle with a little fleur de sel. Serve immediately.

COOK'S TIP
Fleur de sel is available in large supermarkets, health food stores, or online. You can use sea salt, such as Maldon sea salt, instead.

Nutritional information: Energy 384kcal/1623kJ; Protein 7g; Carbohydrate 61g, of which sugars 40g; Fat 14g, of which saturates 9g; Cholesterol 59mg; Calcium 198mg; Fibre 1.4g; Sodium 713mg.

Walnut chocolate crunch whoopie pies

These whoopie pies are deliciously moist, moreish and crunchy with a rich chocolate base. They make the perfect combination for chocoholics and nut fanatics alike. To finish them off perfectly they are drizzled decadently with dulce de leche.

MAKES 12 WHOOPIE PIES

For the cakes
130g/4½oz/generous ½ cup unsalted butter, softened
150g/5oz/¾ cup caster (superfine) sugar
seeds of 1 vanilla pod (bean)
1 egg
300g/11oz/2¾ cups plain (all-purpose) flour
40g/1½oz unsweetened cocoa powder
7.5ml/1½ tsp bicarbonate of soda (baking soda)
5ml/1 tsp salt
50ml/2fl oz/¼ cup milk
150ml/¼ pint/⅔ cup buttermilk
100g/3¾oz/scant 1 cup walnuts, chopped

For the filling
250ml/8fl oz/1 cup double (heavy) cream
45ml/3 tbsp dulce de leche

For the topping and decoration
175ml/6fl oz/¾ cup dulce de leche
12 walnut halves

1 Preheat the oven to 180°C/350°F/ Gas 4. Line two baking trays with baking parchment or silicone mats.

2 For the cakes, whisk the butter, sugar and vanilla seeds together until light and creamy. Whisk in the egg. In a separate bowl, sift the flour with the cocoa powder, bicarbonate of soda and salt.

3 Fold half of the dry ingredients into the butter mixture. Mix in the milk and buttermilk, then the rest of the dry ingredients. Fold in the walnuts.

4 Using a piping (pastry) bag fitted with a large plain nozzle, pipe 12 5cm/2in rounds of cake mixture (batter) 5cm/2in apart on each baking tray. Bake for 12–15 minutes, or until the cakes bounce back when pressed. Transfer to a wire rack to cool.

5 For the filling, whip the cream until stiff peaks form. Whisk in the dulce de leche. Using a piping bag fitted with a star-shaped nozzle, pipe some filling on to the flat side of one cake and top with the flat side of another. Repeat to make 12 pies. Drizzle a tablespoon of dulce de leche over the top of each pie and decorate with a walnut half.

Nutritional information: Energy 545kcal/2285kJ; Protein 9g; Carbohydrate 55g, of which sugars 35g; Fat 34g, of which saturates 16g; Cholesterol 86mg; Calcium 193mg; Fibre 1.6g; Sodium 408mg.

Nougat nut whoopie pies

A winning combination, the marshmallow filling is given a nougat twist for a light, nutty filling in these tempting whoopie pies. Choose the brightest coloured pistachios you can find for the topping, to create a striking contrast and a pretty finish.

MAKES 12 WHOOPIE PIES

For the cakes
150g/5oz/10 tbsp unsalted
   butter, softened
150g/5oz/generous ½ cup soft light
   brown sugar
50g/2oz/¼ cup caster
   (superfine) sugar
seeds of 1 vanilla pod (bean)
2 eggs
350g/12oz/3 cups plain
   (all-purpose) flour
7.5ml/1½ tsp bicarbonate of soda
   (baking soda)
5ml/1 tsp salt
150ml/¼ pint/⅔ cup buttermilk

For the nougat filling
50ml/2fl oz/¼ cup boiling water
15g/½oz powdered gelatine
175g/6oz/generous ¾ cup caster
   (superfine) sugar
75ml/2½fl oz/⅓ cup golden
   (light corn) syrup
25ml/1½ tbsp cold water
50g/2oz/⅓ cup shelled pistachios,
   roughly chopped

For the topping
150g/5oz/1¼ cups icing
   (confectioners') sugar
25ml/1½ tbsp cold water
25g/1oz/¼ cup shelled pistachios,
   finely chopped

1 Preheat the oven to 180°C/350°F/ Gas 4. Line two baking trays with baking parchment or silicone mats. For the cakes, beat the butter, sugars and vanilla seeds together until creamy. Beat in the eggs, one at a time.

2 In a separate bowl, sift the flour with the bicarbonate of soda and salt. Fold half of the dry ingredients into the butter mixture. Mix in the buttermilk, then the rest of the dry ingredients.

3 Using a piping (pastry) bag fitted with a large plain nozzle, pipe 12 5cm/2in rounds of cake mixture (batter) 5cm/2in apart on each baking tray. Bake for 12–15 minutes, or until the cakes bounce back when gently pressed. Transfer to a wire rack to cool.

4 To make the filling, place the boiling water in the bowl of an electric mixer and sprinkle with the gelatine. Whisk on low speed until the gelatine dissolves. In a deep pan, mix the sugar, golden syrup and cold water together and heat until the mixture comes to a rolling boil, stirring.

5 With the electric mixer still on low speed, gradually pour the hot sugar syrup into the mixing bowl containing the gelatine mixture, being careful not to let the hot liquid splash. Once all the sugar syrup has been added to the gelatine mixture, turn the mixer to high speed and whisk for about 5 minutes or until the mixture turns very thick, pale and fluffy. Fold in the pistachios.

6 To make the icing, mix the icing sugar and water together in a small bowl to form a smooth, thick paste.

7 Place a tablespoonful of filling on to the flat side of one cake and top with the flat side of another. Repeat to make 12 pies. Spread a little icing over the top of each pie, then sprinkle with chopped pistachios.

Nutritional information: Energy 441kcal/1866kJ; Protein 7g; Carbohydrate 74g, of which sugars 52g; Fat 15g, of which saturates 8g; Cholesterol 68mg; Calcium 84mg; Fibre 1.1g; Sodium 385mg.

Rich and indulgent whoopies

Decadent ingredients fill the pages of this chapter, from gold leaf pieces and edible glitter to dulce de leche and honeycomb ice cream. There are plenty of grown-up treats to try, such as Tiramisu Whoopie Pies, which are rich and full of creamy coffee deliciousness. For something really sticky and sweet, try the Mini Jam Doughnut Whoopie Pies, which encase their jammy secret inside a hidden hollow, or the ultra gooey Chocolate Date Whoopie Pies.

Mini jam doughnut whoopie pies

Made to resemble jam doughnuts, these mini whoopie pies are innovative and fun. They hide their strawberry jam surprise inside the cakes, just like a real jam doughnut. Try using different jams such as peach, apricot or raspberry. A real winner, whatever the jam!

MAKES 24 WHOOPIE PIES

For the cakes
150g/5oz/10 tbsp unsalted
   butter, softened
150g/5oz/generous ½ cup soft light
   brown sugar
50g/2oz/¼ cup caster
   (superfine) sugar
seeds of 1 vanilla pod (bean)
2 eggs
350g/12oz/3 cups plain
   (all-purpose) flour
7.5ml/1½ tsp bicarbonate of soda
   (baking soda)
5ml/1 tsp salt
150ml/¼ pint/⅔ cup buttermilk

For the filling
300g/11oz/generous 1 cup
   strawberry jam

For the icing and decoration
150g/5oz/1¼ cups icing
   (confectioners') sugar
25ml/1½ tbsp cold water
25g/1oz/2 tbsp granulated (white)
   sugar, for sprinkling

1 Preheat the oven to 180°C/350°F/ Gas 4. Line two baking trays with baking parchment or silicone mats. Whisk the butter, sugars and vanilla seeds together until light and creamy. Whisk in the eggs, one at a time.

2 In a separate bowl, sift the flour with the bicarbonate of soda and salt. Fold half of the dry ingredients into the butter mixture. Mix in the buttermilk, then the rest of the dry ingredients.

3 Using a piping (pastry) bag fitted with a large plain nozzle, pipe 24 3cm/ 1¼in rounds of cake mixture (batter) 4cm/1½in apart on each baking tray. Bake for 10–12 minutes, until golden. Transfer to a wire rack to cool. Meanwhile, mix the icing sugar and water together to make a smooth icing.

4 Scoop out about a teaspoon of cake from the flat side of two cakes. Fill the holes with jam and sandwich them together. Repeat to make 24 pies.

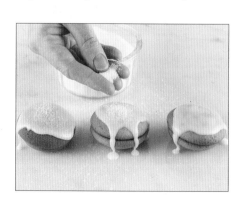

5 Spread a little icing over the top of each pie and sprinkle with sugar.

Nutritional information: Energy 191kcal/809kJ; Protein 3g; Carbohydrate 37g, of which sugars 26g; Fat 5g, of which saturates 3g; Cholesterol 32mg; Calcium 37mg; Fibre 0.7g; Sodium 169mg.

Golden whoopie pies

Show off with these decadent whoopie pies when a special occasion calls for something luxurious. They are flecked with saffron threads and filled with a rich honey-flavoured buttercream. The exquisite look is completed with a sprinkle of golden glitter and gold leaf.

MAKES 12 WHOOPIE PIES

For the cakes
35 saffron threads
15ml/1 tbsp boiling water
130g/4½oz/generous ½ cup unsalted butter, softened
150g/5oz/¾ cup caster (superfine) sugar
seeds of 1 vanilla pod (bean)
1 egg
350g/12oz/3 cups plain (all-purpose) flour
7.5ml/1½ tsp bicarbonate of soda (baking soda)
5ml/1 tsp salt
150ml/¼ pint/⅔ cup buttermilk
50ml/2fl oz/¼ cup milk

For the filling
2 egg whites
125g/4¼oz/generous ½ cup caster (superfine) sugar
225g/8oz/1 cup unsalted butter, softened
45ml/3 tbsp clear honey

For the icing and decoration
150g/5oz/1¼ cups icing (confectioners') sugar
25ml/1½ tbsp cold water
25g/1oz edible golden glitter
12 small edible gold leaf pieces

1 Preheat the oven to 180°C/350°F/ Gas 4. Line two baking trays with baking parchment or silicone mats. For the cakes, tear the saffron threads, place them in a cup and add the boiling water. Stir, then set aside. Whisk the butter, sugar and vanilla seeds together until light and fluffy. Whisk in the egg.

2 In a separate bowl, sift the flour with the bicarbonate of soda and salt. Fold half of the dry ingredients into the butter mixture. Mix in the buttermilk and milk, then the remaining dry ingredients. Fold in the saffron water.

3 Using a piping (pastry) bag fitted with a large plain nozzle, pipe 12 5cm/ 2in rounds of cake mixture (batter) 5cm/2in apart on each baking tray. Bake for 12–15 minutes, or until the cakes bounce back when pressed. Transfer to a wire rack to cool.

4 For the filling, put the egg whites and sugar in a heatproof bowl set over a pan of gently simmering water. Using an electric whisk, whisk the ingredients together until the sugar has dissolved and the mixture is white and hot. Remove from the heat and continue to whisk on high speed until the bowl starts to cool down. Turn the speed to low and whisk in the butter, a little at a time. Gently fold in the honey.

5 To make the icing, mix the icing sugar and water together in a small bowl to form a smooth, thick paste.

6 To assemble the pies, using a piping bag fitted with a star-shaped nozzle, pipe some filling on to the flat side of one cake and top with the flat side of another. Repeat to make 12 pies. Spread a little icing over the top of each pie. Sprinkle with golden glitter and top each with a piece of gold leaf.

Nutritional information: Energy 536kcal/2265kJ; Protein 5g; Carbohydrate 77g, of which sugars 54g; Fat 26g, of which saturates 16g; Cholesterol 88mg; Calcium 72mg; Fibre 1.1g; Sodium 335mg.

Milk and honey whoopie pies

These whoopie pies look attractive drizzled with honey and topped with crumbled honeycomb. They are perfect for a mid-morning snack or for a quick afternoon energy boost. You can make the honeycomb yourself, if you like, or break up some store-bought honeycomb, if pressed for time.

3 Using a piping (pastry) bag fitted with a large plain nozzle, pipe 12 5cm/2in rounds of cake mixture (batter) 5cm/2in apart on each of the baking trays. Bake for 12–15 minutes, or until the cakes bounce back when gently pressed. Transfer to a wire rack and leave to cool.

4 To make the filling, pour the cream into a bowl, add the honey and whisk together until stiff peaks form.

5 To assemble the pies, place a tablespoonful of whipped cream filling on to the flat side of one cake and top with the flat side of another cake. Repeat to make 12 pies.

6 Drizzle the top of each pie with a teaspoonful of honey, then decorate with a piece of honeycomb.

MAKES 12 WHOOPIE PIES

For the cakes
125g/4¼oz/8½ tbsp unsalted
  butter, softened
175g/6oz/¾ cup soft light
  brown sugar
seeds of 1 vanilla pod (bean)
1 egg
350g/12oz/3 cups plain
  (all-purpose) flour
7.5ml/1½ tsp bicarbonate of soda
  (baking soda)
5ml/1 tsp salt
250ml/8fl oz/1 cup buttermilk
45ml/3 tbsp clear honey

For the filling
250ml/8fl oz/1 cup whipping cream
45ml/3 tbsp clear honey

For the topping and decoration
60ml/4 tbsp clear honey
12 small pieces of honeycomb
  (see recipe on page 61)

1 Preheat the oven to 180°C/350°F/ Gas 4. Line two baking trays with baking parchment or silicone mats.

2 For the cakes, whisk the butter, sugar and vanilla seeds together until light and creamy. Whisk in the egg. In a separate bowl, sift the flour with the bicarbonate of soda and salt. In a measuring jug (cup), stir the buttermilk and honey together. Fold half of the dry ingredients into the butter mixture. Mix in the buttermilk mixture, then the rest of the dry ingredients.

Nutritional information: Energy 335kcal/1420kJ; Protein 5g; Carbohydrate 61g, of which sugars 39g; Fat 10g, of which saturates 6g; Cholesterol 45mg; Calcium 105mg; Fibre 1.1g; Sodium 364mg.

Runny honey whoopie pies

Fragrant but not overly sweet, these whoopie pies will be a favourite for honey lovers everywhere. The light buttercream filling is delicate and sumptuous at the same time, but you could always substitute any of the other honey-based fillings in this book, if you like.

MAKES 12 WHOOPIE PIES

For the cakes
125g/4¼oz/8½ tbsp unsalted
    butter, softened
175g/6oz/¾ cup soft light
    brown sugar
seeds of 1 vanilla pod (bean)
1 egg
350g/12oz/3 cups plain
    (all-purpose) flour
7.5ml/1½ tsp bicarbonate of soda
    (baking soda)
5ml/1 tsp salt
250ml/8fl oz/1 cup buttermilk
30ml/2 tbsp clear honey

For the buttercream filling
300g/11oz/2¾ cups icing
    (confectioners') sugar
seeds of 1 vanilla pod (bean)
165g/5½oz/scant ¾ cup unsalted
    butter, softened
90ml/6 tbsp double (heavy) cream
45ml/3 tbsp clear honey

For the topping
60ml/4 tbsp clear honey

1 Preheat the oven to 180°C/350°F/ Gas 4. Line two baking trays with baking parchment or silicone mats.

2 For the cakes, whisk the butter, sugar and vanilla seeds together until light and creamy. Whisk in the egg. In a separate bowl, sift the flour with the bicarbonate of soda and salt. Fold half of the dry ingredients into the butter mixture. Mix in the buttermilk, then the rest of the dry ingredients. Fold in the honey, mixing well.

3 Using a piping (pastry) bag fitted with a large plain nozzle, pipe 12 5cm/2in rounds of cake mixture (batter) 5cm/2in apart on each of the baking trays. Bake for 12–15 minutes, or until the cakes bounce back when gently pressed. Transfer to a wire rack to cool.

4 To make the filling, place the icing sugar, vanilla seeds and butter in a bowl. Using an electric whisk on medium speed, whisk the ingredients together until lightly crumbly. Slowly whisk in the cream, then increase the speed to high and whisk until the mixture is creamy and smooth.

5 Mix in the honey until combined. Using a piping bag fitted with a star-shaped nozzle, pipe some filling on to the flat side of one cake and top with the flat side of another. Repeat to make 12 pies. Drizzle a teaspoonful of honey over each pie.

Nutritional information: Energy 529kcal/2234kJ; Protein 5g; Carbohydrate 75g, of which sugars 53g; Fat 25g, of which saturates 16g; Cholesterol 87mg; Calcium 111mg; Fibre 1.1g; Sodium 369mg.

Chocolate nut whoopie pies

Moist and nutty chocolate cakes are sandwiched together with a silky chocolate hazelnut filling, and topped with melted dark chocolate to create these indulgent whoopie pies. The cake mixture is quite thick and chunky, so it is best to use an ice cream scoop to form the cake rounds.

MAKES 12 WHOOPIE PIES

130g/4½oz/generous ½ cup unsalted
  butter, softened
150g/5oz/¾ cup caster
  (superfine) sugar
seeds of 1 vanilla pod (bean)
1 egg
300g/11oz/2¾ cups plain
  (all-purpose) flour
25g/1oz unsweetened cocoa powder
7.5ml/1½ tsp bicarbonate of soda
  (baking soda)
5ml/1 tsp salt
100g/3¾oz/scant 1 cup dry roasted
  unsalted peanuts, roughly chopped
150ml/¼ pint/⅔ cup buttermilk
50ml/2fl oz/¼ cup milk
300g/11oz chocolate hazelnut spread

For the topping
100g/3¾oz dark (bittersweet)
  chocolate, melted
50g/2oz/½ cup chopped hazelnuts

1 Preheat the oven to 180°C/350°F/
Gas 4. Line two baking trays with
baking parchment or silicone mats.

2 Whisk the butter, sugar and vanilla
seeds together until light and creamy.
Whisk in the egg.

3 In a separate bowl, sift the flour with
the cocoa powder, bicarbonate of soda
and salt, then stir in the peanuts. Fold
half of the flour mixture into the butter
mixture. Mix in the buttermilk and
milk, then the rest of the flour mixture.

4 Using an ice cream scoop or 2
tablespoons, scoop or spoon 12
5cm/2in rounds of cake mixture
(batter) 5cm/2in apart on each of the
baking trays. Bake for 12–15
minutes, or until the cakes bounce
back when gently pressed. Transfer
to a wire rack and leave to cool
completely before assembling.

5 To assemble the pies, place about
2 tablespoonfuls of the chocolate
hazelnut spread on the flat side of
one cake and top with the flat side of
another. Repeat with the remaining
cakes and filling to make 12 pies.

6 Spoon a little melted chocolate on
to the top of each pie, spreading the
chocolate evenly with the back of
the spoon. Lightly sprinkle each pie
with chopped hazelnuts.

Nutritional information: Energy 467kcal/1964kJ; Protein 6g; Carbohydrate 58g, of which sugars 39g; Fat 25g, of which saturates 8g; Cholesterol 46mg; Calcium 74mg; Fibre 1.3g; Sodium 357mg.

Pecan whoopie pies

The American classic pecan pie is given a makeover in this recipe, which takes the traditional flavours and uses them to create a fluffy whoopie pie with rich, buttery pecan nuts. The simple whipped cream and maple syrup filling complements the pecans beautifully.

MAKES 12 WHOOPIE PIES

For the cakes
125g/4¼oz/8½ tbsp unsalted
   butter, softened
175g/6oz/¾ cup soft light
   brown sugar
seeds of 1 vanilla pod (bean)
1 egg
350g/12oz/3 cups plain
   (all-purpose) flour
7.5ml/1½ tsp bicarbonate of soda
   (baking soda)
5ml/1 tsp salt
250ml/8fl oz/1 cup buttermilk
90g/3½oz/scant 1 cup pecan nuts,
   roughly chopped

For the filling
250ml/8fl oz/1 cup double
   (heavy) cream
45ml/3 tbsp maple syrup

For the topping and decoration
200g/7oz dulce de leche
12 pecan halves

1 Preheat the oven to 180°C/350°F/ Gas 4. Line two baking trays with baking parchment or silicone mats.

2 To make the cakes, whisk the butter, brown sugar and vanilla seeds together until light and creamy. Whisk in the egg.

3 In a separate bowl, sift the flour with the bicarbonate of soda and salt. Fold half of the dry ingredients into the butter mixture. Mix in the buttermilk, then the remainder of the dry ingredients.

4 Fold in the chopped pecans, mixing well.

5 Using an ice cream scoop or 2 tablespoons, scoop or spoon 12 5cm/2in rounds of cake mixture (batter) 5cm/2in apart on each of the baking trays. Bake for 12–15 minutes, or until the cakes bounce back when gently pressed. Transfer to a wire rack and leave to cool.

6 For the filling, whip the cream until stiff peaks form. Add the maple syrup and whisk to combine.

7 Place a tablespoonful of filling on to the flat side of one cake and top with the flat side of another. Repeat to make 12 pies. Spread a tablespoonful of dulce de leche over the top of each pie and decorate each with a pecan half.

Nutritional information: Energy 562kcal/2356kJ; Protein 9g; Carbohydrate 61g, of which sugars 38g; Fat 34g, of which saturates 16g; Cholesterol 84mg; Calcium 196mg; Fibre 1.1g; Sodium 378mg.

Banoffee and walnut whoopie pies

Banoffee pie is a classic flavour combination, ideal for the super sweet-toothed! Whipped cream for the filling balances the sweetness of the caramel. Another nutty cake mixture, you will probably find it easier to scoop or spoon the mixture on to baking trays than to pipe it.

4 Fold in the mashed bananas and walnuts, mixing well.

5 Using an ice cream scoop or two tablespoons, scoop or spoon 12 5cm/2in rounds of cake mixture (batter) 5cm/2in apart on each baking tray. Bake for 12–15 minutes, or until the cakes bounce back when gently pressed. Transfer to a wire rack to cool.

6 To make the filling, whip the cream until stiff peaks form. Fold in the dulce de leche.

7 Using a piping (pastry) bag fitted with a star-shaped nozzle, pipe some whipped cream filling on to the flat side of one cake and top with the flat side of another. Repeat to make 12 pies.

MAKES 12 WHOOPIE PIES

For the cakes
130g/4½oz/generous ½ cup
  unsalted butter, softened
150g/5oz/generous ½ cup soft light
  brown sugar
1 egg, beaten
300g/11oz/2¾ cups plain
  (all-purpose) flour
7.5ml/1½ tsp bicarbonate of soda
  (baking soda)
5ml/1 tsp salt
2.5ml/½ tsp ground cinnamon
a pinch of freshly grated nutmeg
50ml/2fl oz/¼ cup milk
150ml/¼ pint/⅔ cup buttermilk
200g/7oz mashed bananas
40g/1½oz/scant ½ cup walnuts,
  roughly chopped

For the filling
150ml/¼ pint/⅔ cup double
  (heavy) cream
100g/3¾oz dulce de leche

1 Preheat the oven to 180°C/350°F/ Gas 4. Line two baking trays with baking parchment or silicone mats.

2 For the cakes, whisk the butter and brown sugar together until light and fluffy. Whisk in the egg.

3 In a separate bowl, sift the flour with the bicarbonate of soda, salt, cinnamon and nutmeg. Fold half of the dry ingredients into the butter mixture. Mix in the milk and buttermilk, then the remainder of the dry ingredients.

Nutritional information: Energy 382kcal/1604kJ; Protein 6g; Carbohydrate 46g, of which sugars 27g; Fat 21g, of which saturates 12g; Cholesterol 68mg; Calcium 127mg; Fibre 1.6g; Sodium 349mg.

Tiramisu whoopie pies

This take on the Italian classic can be made in advance as the flavours will improve as they infuse. Wrap them in clear film (plastic wrap) and refrigerate for up to 2 days. When ready to serve, bring them back to room temperature and dust with cocoa powder – great for a dinner-party dessert!

MAKES 12 WHOOPIE PIES

For the cakes
125g/4¼oz/8½ tbsp unsalted
   butter, softened
175g/6oz/¾ cup soft light
   brown sugar
seeds of 1 vanilla pod (bean)
1 egg
350g/12oz/3 cups plain
   (all-purpose) flour
7.5ml/1½ tsp bicarbonate of soda
   (baking soda)
5ml/1 tsp salt
250ml/8fl oz/1 cup buttermilk
60ml/4 tbsp instant coffee granules
   dissolved in 15ml/1 tbsp hot water

For the mascarpone filling
250ml/8fl oz/1 cup double
   (heavy) cream
200g/7oz/scant 1 cup mascarpone
65g/2½oz/5 tbsp caster
   (superfine) sugar
50ml/2fl oz/¼ cup Marsala (optional)

unsweetened cocoa powder,
   for dusting

1 Preheat the oven to 180°C/350°F/ Gas 4. Line two baking trays with baking parchment or silicone mats.

2 To make the cakes, place the butter in a bowl with the brown sugar and vanilla seeds and whisk together until light and fluffy. Whisk in the egg.

3 In a separate bowl, sift the flour with the bicarbonate of soda and salt. In a measuring jug (cup), mix together the buttermilk and dissolved coffee.

4 Fold half of the dry ingredients into the butter mixture. Mix in the buttermilk mixture, then the remainder of the dry ingredients.

5 Using a piping (pastry) bag fitted with a large plain nozzle, pipe 12 5cm/2in rounds of cake mixture (batter) 5cm/2in apart on each baking tray. Bake for 12–15 minutes, or until the cakes bounce back when pressed. Transfer to a wire rack to cool.

6 For the filling, whisk the cream, mascarpone, sugar and Marsala (if using) together until stiff peaks form.

7 Using a piping bag fitted with a star-shaped nozzle, pipe some filling on to the flat side of one cake and top with the flat side of another. Repeat to make 12 pies. Dust the top of each pie with cocoa powder.

Nutritional information: Energy 446kcal/1870kJ; Protein 6g; Carbohydrate 46g, of which sugars 23g; Fat 28g, of which saturates 18g; Cholesterol 90mg; Calcium 107mg; Fibre 1.1 g; Sodium 342mg.

Chocolate passion whoopie pies

Not an everyday flavour combination, these whoopie pies are sure to be a surprising delight. They combine a rich chocolatey buttercream with a zingy passion-fruit glaze, and this sweet and sour combination contrasts beautifully with the light chocolate cakes.

MAKES 12 WHOOPIE PIES

For the cakes
150g/5oz/10 tbsp unsalted
  butter, softened
150g/5oz/generous ½ cup soft
  light brown sugar
50g/2oz/¼ cup caster
  (superfine) sugar
seeds of 1 vanilla pod (bean)
2 eggs
350g/12oz/3 cups plain
  (all-purpose) flour
50g/2oz unsweetened
  cocoa powder
7.5ml/1½ tsp bicarbonate of soda
  (baking soda)
5ml/1 tsp salt
150ml/¼ pint/⅔ cup buttermilk
50ml/2fl oz/¼ cup milk

For the buttercream filling
300g/11oz/2¾ cups icing
  (confectioners') sugar
seeds of 1 vanilla pod (bean)
150g/5oz/10 tbsp unsalted
  butter, softened
90ml/6 tbsp double (heavy) cream
40g/1½oz unsweetened cocoa powder

For the glaze and decoration
90ml/6 tbsp icing
  (confectioners') sugar
juice of 2 passion fruits
chocolate sprinkles

1 Preheat the oven to 180°C/350°F/ Gas 4. Line two baking trays with baking parchment or silicone mats. For the cakes, whisk the butter, sugars and vanilla until fluffy. Whisk in the eggs.

2 In a separate bowl, sift the flour with the cocoa powder, bicarbonate of soda and salt. Fold half of the dry ingredients into the butter mixture. Mix in the buttermilk and milk, then the remainder of the dry ingredients.

3 Using a piping (pastry) bag fitted with a large plain nozzle, pipe 12 5cm/2in rounds of cake mixture (batter) 5cm/2in apart on each baking tray. Bake for 12–15 minutes, or until the cakes bounce back when pressed. Transfer to a wire rack to cool.

4 For the filling, whisk the icing sugar, vanilla seeds and butter together, using an electric whisk on medium speed, until crumbly. Slowly whisk in the cream, then increase the speed to high and whisk until creamy and smooth. Fold in the cocoa powder.

5 For the glaze, mix the icing sugar and passion fruit juice together to form a smooth paste. Using a piping bag fitted with a plain nozzle, pipe some filling on to the flat side of one cake and top with the flat side of another. Repeat to make 12 pies. Roll the edges of the filling in sprinkles, then drizzle the tops of the pies with the glaze.

Nutritional information: Energy 554kcal/2340kJ; Protein 6g; Carbohydrate 75g, of which sugars 51g; Fat 28g, of which saturates 17g; Cholesterol 107mg; Calcium 92mg; Fibre 1.1g; Sodium 409mg.

Chocolate date whoopie pies

Sumptuous and rich, these unusual whoopie pies are for those with a really sweet tooth. Fluffy chocolate cakes with chunks of chewy dates are sandwiched together by a sticky dulce de leche filling, which oozes out when you take your first bite. A truly satisfying mouthful!

MAKES 12 WHOOPIE PIES

125g/4¼oz/8½ tbsp unsalted
   butter, softened
175g/6oz/¾ cup soft light
   brown sugar
seeds of 1 vanilla pod (bean)
1 egg
300g/11oz/2¾ cup plain
   (all-purpose) flour
50g/2oz unsweetened
   cocoa powder
7.5ml/1½ tsp bicarbonate of soda
   (baking soda)
5ml/1 tsp salt
75g/3oz/½ cup dates, stoned
   (pitted) and chopped
250ml/8fl oz/1 cup buttermilk
200g/7oz dulce de leche
icing (confectioners') sugar,
   for dusting

1 Preheat the oven to 180°C/350°F/ Gas 4. Line two baking trays with baking parchment or silicone mats. Whisk the butter, brown sugar and vanilla seeds until light and fluffy. Add the egg and whisk well.

2 In a separate bowl, sift the flour with the cocoa powder, bicarbonate of soda and salt, then stir in the dates.

3 Fold the flour mixture into the butter mixture in three stages, alternating each addition with the buttermilk, until all of the flour mixture and the buttermilk have been encorporated.

4 Using a piping (pastry) bag fitted with a large plain nozzle, pipe 12 5cm/2in rounds of cake mixture (batter) 5cm/2in apart on each baking tray. Bake for 12–15 minutes, or until the cakes bounce back when pressed. Transfer to a wire rack and leave to cool completely.

5 Spread a tablespoonful of dulce de leche on to the flat side of one cake and cover with the flat side of another. Repeat to make 12 pies. Dust with sifted icing sugar.

Nutritional information: Energy 327kcal/1384kJ; Protein 5g; Carbohydrate 57g, of which sugars 37g; Fat 11g, of which saturates 7g; Cholesterol 45mg; Calcium 78mg; Fibre 0.9g; Sodium 379mg.

Triple chocolate whoopie pies

This is the perfect combination for all chocoholics – a rich, dense and moreish chocolate mix that resembles a mini chocolate layer cake. Try them with chocolate chips for an extra chocolate kick, or melt white or milk chocolate on top for a different effect – or even use a mixture of all three.

2 In a separate bowl, sift the flour with the cocoa powder, bicarbonate of soda and salt. Fold half of the dry ingredients into the butter mixture. Mix in the milk and buttermilk, then the remaining dry ingredients. Using a piping (pastry) bag fitted with a large plain nozzle, pipe 12 5cm/2in rounds of cake mixture (batter) 5cm/2in apart on each baking tray. Bake for 12–15 minutes, or until the cakes bounce back when pressed. Transfer to a wire rack to cool.

3 For the filling, put the egg whites and sugar in a heatproof bowl over a pan of simmering water. With an electric whisk, whisk until the sugar has dissolved and the mixture is white and hot. Remove from the heat and continue to whisk on high speed until the bowl starts to cool. Turn the speed to low and whisk in the butter, a little at a time. Gently fold in the cocoa powder. Refrigerate the filling for 30 minutes–1 hour, until thickened.

MAKES 12 WHOOPIE PIES

For the cakes
150g/5oz/10 tbsp unsalted
  butter, softened
150g/5oz/generous ½ cup soft light
  brown sugar
50g/2oz/¼ cup caster (superfine)
  sugar
seeds of 1 vanilla pod (bean)
2 eggs
350g/12oz/3 cups plain
  (all-purpose) flour
50g/2oz unsweetened cocoa powder
7.5ml/1½ tsp bicarbonate of soda
  (baking soda)
5ml/1 tsp salt
150ml/¼ pint/⅔ cup buttermilk
50ml/2fl oz/¼ cup milk

For the filling
2 egg whites
125g/4¼oz/generous ½ cup caster
  (superfine) sugar
225g/8oz/1 cup unsalted
  butter, softened
40g/1½oz unsweetened cocoa powder

For the topping
100g/3¾oz dark (bittersweet)
  chocolate, melted
dark chocolate chips

1 Preheat the oven to 180°C/350°F/Gas 4. Line two baking trays with baking parchment or silicone mats. For the cakes, whisk the butter, sugars and vanilla seeds together until fluffy. Whisk in the eggs, one at a time.

4 Using a piping bag fitted with a star-shaped nozzle, pipe chocolate filling on to the flat side of one cake and top with the flat side of another. Repeat to make 12 pies. Spread melted chocolate on the tops and decorate with chocolate chips.

Nutritional information: Energy 463kcal/1951kJ; Protein 7g; Carbohydrate 58g, of which sugars 34g; Fat 25g, of which saturates 15g; Cholesterol 92mg; Calcium 92mg; Fibre 1.1g; Sodium 414mg.

Mississippi mud whoopie pies

A chocoholic's delight, these whoopie pies combine rich chocolate cakes with a filling of good quality dark chocolate ice cream. They are based on the chocolatey flavours of the classic American dessert, but contain a novel ice cream filling. Only fill them with ice cream when you are ready to serve them.

MAKES 12 WHOOPIE PIES

125g/4¼oz/8½ tbsp unsalted
  butter, softened
175g/6oz/¾ cup soft light
  brown sugar
seeds of 1 vanilla pod (bean)
1 egg
300g/11oz/2¾ cups plain
  (all-purpose) flour
50g/2oz unsweetened cocoa powder
7.5ml/1½ tsp bicarbonate of soda
  (baking soda)
5ml/1 tsp salt
250ml/8fl oz/1 cup buttermilk
400ml/14fl oz/1⅔ cups dark
  chocolate ice cream
150g/5oz dark (bittersweet)
  chocolate, melted
sprinkles, to decorate

1 Preheat the oven to 180°C/350°F/ Gas 4. Line two baking trays with baking parchment or silicone mats.

2 For the cakes, whisk the butter, brown sugar and vanilla seeds together until light and creamy. Whisk in the egg.

3 In a separate bowl, sift the flour with the cocoa powder, bicarbonate of soda and salt. Fold half of the dry ingredients into the butter mixture.

COOK'S TIP
Try toasting the cakes just before sandwiching them with the ice cream. Drizzle with the melted chocolate and serve warm.

4 Mix in the buttermilk, then add the remainder of the dry ingredients and mix until fully incorporated.

5 Using a piping (pastry) bag fitted with a large plain nozzle, pipe 12 5cm/2in rounds of cake mixture (batter) 5cm/2in apart on each baking tray. Bake for 12–15 minutes, or until the cakes bounce back when pressed. Transfer to a wire rack to cool.

6 Meanwhile, and only when you are ready to serve the whoopie pies, remove the ice cream from the freezer, measure it into a bowl or container and leave it to soften for 10 minutes.

7 Using an ice cream scoop, place a scoopful of ice cream on to the flat side of one cake and top with the flat side of another. Smooth the edge of the ice cream with a knife. Repeat to make 12 pies. Drizzle melted chocolate over the tops and decorate with sprinkles.

Nutritional information: Energy 367kcal/1549kJ; Protein 6g; Carbohydrate 52g, of which sugars 32g; Fat 17g, of which saturates 10g; Cholesterol 53mg; Calcium 119mg; Fibre 0.9g; Sodium 387mg.

Ice cream sandwich whoopie pies

Cool and refreshing, these whoopie pies are the perfect indulgence on a hot summer's day. Filled with chocolate ice cream, they should be assembled just before serving. They look fantastic when dipped in melted chocolate, but this can be a race against time before the ice cream melts!

MAKES 12 WHOOPIE PIES

125g/4¼oz/8½ tbsp unsalted
  butter, softened
175g/6oz/¾ cup soft light
  brown sugar
seeds of 1 vanilla pod (bean)
1 egg
350g/12oz/3 cups plain
  (all-purpose) flour
7.5ml/1½ tsp bicarbonate of soda
  (baking soda)
5ml/1 tsp salt
250ml/8fl oz/1 cup buttermilk

For the filling and decoration
400ml/14fl oz/1⅔ cups chocolate
  ice cream
100g/3¾oz milk chocolate, melted
unsweetened cocoa powder,
  to decorate

1 Preheat the oven to 180°C/350°F/ Gas 4. Line two baking trays with baking parchment or silicone mats.

2 Whisk the butter, brown sugar and vanilla seeds together until light and fluffy. Whisk in the egg.

3 In a separate bowl, sift the flour with the bicarbonate of soda and salt. Fold half of the dry ingredients into the butter mixture. Mix in the buttermilk, then the remaining dry ingredients.

4 Using a piping (pastry) bag fitted with a large plain nozzle, pipe 12 5cm/ 2in rounds of cake mixture (batter) 5cm/2in apart on each of the baking trays. Bake for 12–15 minutes, or until the cakes bounce back when gently pressed. Transfer to a wire rack to cool. Meanwhile, and only when you are ready to serve the whoopie pies, remove the ice cream from the freezer, measure it into a bowl or container and leave it to soften for 10 minutes.

5 Place a scoopful of ice cream on to the flat side of one cake and top with the flat side of another. Gently squeeze the cakes together. Repeat, working quickly, to make 12 pies. Dip each pie into the melted chocolate and dust with cocoa powder.

VARIATION
Try raspberry swirl semi-freddo in place of the chocolate ice cream.

Nutritional information: Energy 327kcal/1384kJ; Protein 5g; Carbohydrate 57g, of which sugars 37g; Fat 11g, of which saturates 7g; Cholesterol 45mg; Calcium 78mg; Fibre 0.9g; Sodium 379mg.

Hokey pokey ice cream whoopie pies

The filling for these whoopie pies is made by mixing homemade honeycomb into vanilla ice cream. Hokey pokey ice cream is surprisingly easy to make at home. The leftover honeycomb can be stored in an airtight container for 2 weeks. Try coating it in melted chocolate and allowing to set – delicious!

MAKES 12 WHOOPIE PIES

For the cakes
125g/4¼oz/8½ tbsp unsalted
   butter, softened
175g/6oz/¾ cup soft light
   brown sugar
seeds of 1 vanilla pod (bean)
1 egg
350g/12oz/3 cups plain
   (all-purpose) flour
7.5ml/1½ tsp bicarbonate of soda
   (baking soda)
5ml/1 tsp salt
250ml/8fl oz/1 cup buttermilk

For the honeycomb
200g/7oz/1 cup caster
   (superfine) sugar
45ml/3 tbsp clear honey
15ml/1 tbsp golden (light corn) syrup
20ml/4 tsp cold water
3.75ml/¾ tsp bicarbonate of soda
   (baking soda)

For the filling
450ml/¾ pint/scant 2 cups vanilla
   ice cream
30ml/2 tbsp maple syrup

50ml/2fl oz/¼ cup maple syrup,
   for drizzling

1 Preheat the oven to 180°C/350°F/ Gas 4. Line two baking trays with baking parchment or silicone mats. Grease a separate baking tray. For the cakes, whisk the butter, sugar and vanilla seeds together until light and fluffy. Whisk in the egg. In a separate bowl, sift the flour with the bicarbonate of soda and salt.

2 Fold half of the dry ingredients into the butter mixture. Mix in the buttermilk, then the rest of the dry ingredients. Using a piping (pastry) bag fitted with a large plain nozzle, pipe 12 5cm/2in rounds of cake mixture (batter) 5cm/2in apart on each lined baking tray. Bake for 12–15 minutes, or until the cakes bounce back when pressed. Transfer to a wire rack to cool.

3 To make the honeycomb, put the sugar, honey, golden syrup and water in a heavy pan, bring to a rolling boil and boil for 5 minutes. Remove from the heat, immediately whisk in the bicarbonate of soda and pour the mixture quickly into the greased baking tray; it will bubble and froth. Allow the mixture to cool and set. Once set, break the honeycomb into small chunks and store in an airtight container.

4 For the filling, measure the ice cream into a freezerproof bowl or container and leave it to soften for 10 minutes. Stir in 100g/3¾oz of the honeycomb and the maple syrup, then cover and return to the freezer for at least 30 minutes, or until firm.

5 Place a scoopful of ice cream on to the flat side of one cake and top with the flat side of another. Gently squeeze together, then repeat to make 12 pies. Drizzle each with maple syrup.

Nutritional information: Energy 402kcal/1703kJ; Protein 6g; Carbohydrate 70g, of which sugars 47g; Fat 13g, of which saturates 8g; Cholesterol 53mg; Calcium 120mg; Fibre 1.1g; Sodium 424mg.

Weird and wonderful whoopies

Interesting and unusual ingredients fill these whoopie pies: ground aniseed, grated apples, passion fruit, spicy chilli and cardamom, which are bound to be a great talking point around any dinner table. For something fiery, try the Chocolate and Chilli Whoopie Pies with their sweet ganache filling. For tea lovers, there is a lovely selection of infusions using Earl Grey, jasmine tea or matcha, as well as more exotic combinations, such as the Chai Latte Whoopie Pies.

Bee sting whoopie pies

A bee sting is a German pastry made with yeast and covered with a crunchy almond topping. These whoopie pies are a quick and easy alternative, which have all the flavour but none of the hassle. They are best served warm to fully enjoy their wonderful, sticky gooeyness.

4 Bake for 12–15 minutes, or until the cakes are pale golden. Transfer to a wire rack to cool.

5 To make the filling, whip the cream in a bowl until stiff peaks form, then fold in the cold custard, sugar and vanilla seeds, until fully incorporated into the mixture.

6 Using a piping bag fitted with a star-shaped nozzle, pipe some custard cream filling on to the flat side of one cake and cover with the flat side of another. Repeat with the remaining cakes and custard cream filling to make 12 pies.

MAKES 12 WHOOPIE PIES

For the cakes
125g/4¼oz/8½ tbsp unsalted
   butter, softened
175g/6oz/¾ cup soft light
   brown sugar
seeds of 1 vanilla pod (bean)
1 egg
350g/12oz/3 cups plain
   (all-purpose) flour
7.5ml/1½ tsp bicarbonate of soda
   (baking soda)
5ml/1 tsp salt
250ml/8fl oz/1 cup buttermilk

For the filling
150ml/¼ pint/⅔ cup double
   (heavy) cream
100ml/3½fl oz/ scant ½ cup
   ready-made cold vanilla custard
45ml/3 tbsp caster (superfine) sugar
seeds of 1 vanilla pod (bean)

For the topping
175ml/6fl oz/¾ cup golden (light
   corn) syrup, chilled to thicken
40g/1½oz/generous ¼ cup flaked
   (sliced) almonds, lightly toasted

1 Preheat the oven to 180°C/350°F/ Gas 4. Line two baking trays with baking parchment or silicone mats.

2 For the cakes, whisk the butter, sugar and vanilla seeds until light and fluffy. Whisk in the egg. In a separate bowl, sift the flour with the bicarbonate of soda and salt. Fold half of the dry ingredients into the butter mixture. Mix in the buttermilk, then the rest of the dry ingredients.

3 Using a piping (pastry) bag fitted with a large plain nozzle, pipe 12 5cm/ 2in rounds of cake mixture (batter) 5cm/2in apart on each baking tray.

7 Drizzle a tablespoonful of golden syrup over the top of each whoopie pie, then sprinkle them with toasted flaked almonds.

Nutritional information: Energy 379kcal/1600kJ; Protein 5g; Carbohydrate 56g, of which sugars 33g; Fat 17g, of which saturates 9g; Cholesterol 58mg; Calcium 104mg; Fibre 1.5g; Sodium 373mg.

Apple strudel whoopie pies

Inspired by the Viennese classic, these sweet whoopie pies are a real winter treat, bursting with the flavours of cinnamon and raisin. You could also try the cakes hot from the oven, with some filling spooned over the flat side. Very moreish!

MAKES 12 WHOOPIE PIES

For the cakes
130g/4½oz/generous ½ cup unsalted butter, softened
150g/5oz/generous ½ cup soft light brown sugar
seeds of 1 vanilla pod (bean)
1 egg
300g/11oz/2¾ cups plain (all-purpose) flour
7.5ml/1½ tsp bicarbonate of soda (baking soda)
5ml/1 tsp ground cinnamon
5ml/1 tsp salt
50ml/2fl oz/¼ cup milk
150ml/¼ pint/⅔ cup buttermilk

For the filling
6 eating apples, peeled, cored, coarsely grated and squeezed dry
175g/6oz/scant 1 cup caster (superfine) sugar
seeds of 1 vanilla pod (bean)
100g/3¾oz/⅔ cup raisins
finely grated rind of 1 lemon
finely grated rind of 1 orange
100g/3¾oz/scant ½ cup unsalted butter
60ml/4 tbsp cornflour (cornstarch)

For the topping
200ml/7fl oz/scant 1 cup whipping cream
45ml/3 tbsp caster (superfine) sugar
seeds of 1 vanilla pod (bean)

icing (confectioners') sugar, for dusting

1 Preheat the oven to 180°C/350°F/ Gas 4. Line two baking trays with baking parchment or silicone mats.

2 For the cakes, whisk the butter, sugar and vanilla together. Whisk in the egg.

3 In a separate bowl, sift the flour with the bicarbonate of soda, cinnamon and salt. Fold half of the dry ingredients into the butter mixture. Mix in the milk and buttermilk, then the rest of the dry ingredients. Using a piping (pastry) bag fitted with a large plain nozzle, pipe 12 5cm/2in rounds of mixture (batter) 5cm/2in apart on each baking tray.

4 Bake for 12–15 minutes, or until the cakes bounce back when gently pressed. Transfer to a wire rack to cool.

5 For the filling, mix the grated apples with the sugar, vanilla seeds, raisins and citrus rinds in a bowl. Set aside. Melt the butter in a pan, whisk in the cornflour until smooth, then stir into the filling mixture.

6 For the topping, whip the cream until stiff peaks form, then whisk in the sugar and vanilla seeds.

7 Place a tablespoonful of the filling on to the flat side of one cake and top with the flat side of another. Repeat to make 12 pies. Using a piping bag fitted with a star-shaped nozzle, pipe the topping on to the tops of the whoopie pies, then dust with sifted icing sugar.

Nutritional information: Energy 472kcal/1990kJ; Protein 4g; Carbohydrate 65g, of which sugars 41g; Fat 24g, of which saturates 15g; Cholesterol 82mg; Calcium 89mg; Fibre 2.4g; Sodium 337mg.

Chai latte whoopie pies

These whoopie pies are like a warm and comforting cup of chai latte on a cold winter's day. Definitely one for the grown-ups, these are sure to delight friends who pop round for a cup of tea or coffee. Instant chai latte mixes are available in large supermarkets.

MAKES 12 WHOOPIE PIES

For the cakes
150g/5oz/10 tbsp unsalted
  butter, softened
150g/5oz/generous ½ cup soft light
  brown sugar
50g/2oz/¼ cup caster
  (superfine) sugar
seeds of 1 vanilla pod (bean)
2 eggs
350g/12oz/3 cups plain
  (all-purpose) flour
45ml/3 tbsp instant chai latte powder
7.5ml/1½ tsp bicarbonate of soda
  (baking soda)
5ml/1 tsp salt
150ml/¼ pint/⅔ cup buttermilk

For the filling
200ml/7fl oz/scant 1 cup
  whipping cream
40g/1½oz/2 tbsp caster
  (superfine) sugar
seeds of 1 vanilla pod (bean)

For the topping
100g/3¾oz white chocolate, broken
  into squares
5ml/1 tsp ground cinnamon

1 Preheat the oven to 180°C/350°F/ Gas 4. Line two baking trays with baking parchment or silicone mats. For the cakes, beat the butter, sugars and vanilla seeds together until creamy. Beat in the eggs, one at a time.

2 In a separate bowl, sift the flour with the chai latte, bicarbonate of soda and salt. Fold half of the dry ingredients into the butter mixture. Mix in the buttermilk, then the remainder of the dry ingredients.

3 Using a piping (pastry) bag fitted with a large plain nozzle, pipe 12 5cm/2in rounds of cake mixture (batter) 5cm/2in apart on each baking tray. Bake for 12–15 minutes, or until the cakes bounce back when pressed. Transfer to a wire rack and leave to cool.

4 For the filling, place the cream, sugar and vanilla seeds in a bowl and whip together until stiff peaks form.

5 To make the topping, place the chocolate and cinnamon in a heatproof bowl, set over a pan of simmering water. Stir until melted.

6 Using a piping bag fitted with a small plain nozzle, pipe some of the filling on to the flat side of one cake and top with the flat side of another. Repeat to make 12 pies. Spread a little of the melted chocolate mixture over the top of each pie.

Nutritional information: Energy 362kcal/1523kJ; Protein 5g; Carbohydrate 47g, of which sugars 25g; Fat 19g, of which saturates11g; Cholesterol 86mg; Calcium 81mg; Fibre 1.1g; Sodium 340mg.

Matcha whoopie pies

For green tea fanatics, these whoopie pies are a delight with their health-giving benefits, as they are bursting with antioxidants. They are also a show-stopper due to their bright green colour. Decorate the edges of the sticky marshmallow with sprinkles for a fun look.

MAKES 12 WHOOPIE PIES

For the cakes
130g/4½oz/generous ½ cup unsalted
   butter, softened
150g/5oz/¾ cup caster
   (superfine) sugar
seeds of 1 vanilla pod (bean)
1 egg
325g/11½oz/scant 3 cups plain
   (all-purpose) flour
7.5ml/1½ tsp bicarbonate of soda
   (baking soda)
5ml/1 tsp salt
30ml/2 tbsp matcha green tea powder
150ml/¼ pint/⅔ cup buttermilk
50ml/2fl oz/¼ cup milk

For the marshmallow filling
50ml/2fl oz/¼ cup boiling water
15ml/1 tbsp powdered gelatine
175g/6oz/generous ¾ cup caster
   (superfine) sugar
75ml/2½fl oz/⅓ cup golden
   (light corn) syrup
25ml/1½ tbsp cold water

multicoloured sprinkles, to decorate

1 Preheat the oven to 180°C/350°F/ Gas 4. Line two baking trays with baking parchment or silicone mats. To make the cakes, beat the butter, sugar and vanilla seeds together until light and creamy. Beat in the egg.

2 In a separate bowl, sift the flour with the bicarbonate of soda, salt and matcha powder. Fold half of the dry ingredients into the butter mixture. Mix in the buttermilk and milk, then the remainder of the dry ingredients.

3 Using a piping (pastry) bag fitted with a large plain nozzle, pipe 12 5cm/2in rounds of cake mixture (batter) 5cm/2in apart on each baking tray. Bake for 12–15 minutes, or until the cakes bounce back when gently pressed. Transfer to a wire rack to cool.

4 To make the filling, place the boiling water in the bowl of an electric mixer and sprinkle with the powdered gelatine. Whisk on low speed until the gelatine dissolves. Set aside. In a deep pan, mix the sugar, golden syrup and cold water together and heat until the mixture comes to a rolling boil, stirring. With the electric mixer still on low speed, gradually pour the hot sugar syrup into the mixing bowl containing the gelatine mixture.

5 Turn the electric mixer to high speed and whisk for about 5 minutes or until the mixture is very thick, pale and fluffy.

6 Spread a tablespoonful of filling on to the flat side of one cake and top with the flat side of another. Repeat to make 12 pies. Roll the edges of the marshmallow in sprinkles.

Nutritional information: Energy 308kcal/1305kJ; Protein 4g; Carbohydrate 53g, of which sugars 33g; Fat 10g, of which saturates 6g; Cholesterol 45mg; Calcium 68mg; Fibre1.0g; Sodium 341mg.

Green tea and jasmine whoopie pies

The most famous scented tea in China, jasmine tea is known for its calming effects and is often served to welcome guests. Matcha green tea powder and jasmine extract are available in health food stores, larger supermarkets, online and (often at a lower price) at Chinese and Japanese supermarkets.

2 For the cakes, whisk the butter, sugars and vanilla seeds until light and fluffy. Whisk in the eggs, one at a time. In a separate bowl, sift the flour with the bicarbonate of soda and salt. Fold half of the dry ingredients into the butter mixture. Mix in the buttermilk, then the rest of the dry ingredients. Stir in the jasmine tea and jasmine extract.

3 Using a piping (pastry) bag fitted with a large plain nozzle, pipe 12 5cm/2in rounds of cake mixture (batter) 5cm/2in apart on each baking tray. Bake for 12–15 minutes, or until the cakes bounce back when pressed. Transfer to a wire rack to cool.

4 Whip the filling ingredients together in a bowl until stiff peaks form.

5 For the icing, mix the icing sugar, green tea and matcha powder in a small bowl to form a smooth paste.

6 Using a piping bag fitted with a small star-shaped nozzle, pipe some filling on to the flat side of one cake and top with the flat side of another. Repeat to make 12 pies. Spread a little icing over the top of each pie and sprinkle with extra matcha powder.

MAKES 12 WHOOPIE PIES

For the cakes
150g/5oz/10 tbsp unsalted
  butter, softened
150g/5oz/generous ½ cup soft light
  brown sugar
50g/2oz/¼ cup caster (superfine) sugar
seeds of 1 vanilla pod (bean)
2 eggs
350g/12oz/3 cups plain
  (all-purpose) flour
7.5ml/1½ tsp bicarbonate of soda
  (baking soda)
5ml/1 tsp salt
150ml/¼ pint/⅔ cup buttermilk
15ml/1 tbsp brewed jasmine green tea
4–5 drops jasmine extract

For the filling
250ml/8fl oz/1 cup double
  (heavy) cream
40g/1½oz/3 tbsp caster (superfine)
  sugar
7.5ml/1½ tsp matcha green tea powder

For the icing and decoration
150g/5oz/1¼ cups icing
  (confectioners') sugar
25ml/1½ tbsp brewed cold jasmine
  green tea
5ml/1 tsp matcha green tea powder,
  plus extra for sprinkling

1 Preheat the oven to 180°C/350°F/ Gas 4. Line two baking trays with baking parchment or silicone mats.

Nutritional information: Energy 395kcal/1658kJ; Protein 5g; Carbohydrate 45g, of which sugars 23g; Fat 23g, of which saturates 14g; Cholesterol 97mg; Calcium 82mg; Fibre 1.1g; Sodium 334mg.

Earl sour whoopie pies

With all the taste of an English afternoon tea, these zesty whoopie pies are fresh and uplifting.
The delicate and pretty cakes are flavoured with Earl Grey tea, which is complemented beautifully
by the citrus whipped cream filling and the zingy lemon icing.

MAKES 12 WHOOPIE PIES

For the cakes
1 Earl Grey teabag
30ml/2 tbsp boiling water
130g/4½oz/generous ½ cup unsalted
   butter, softened
150g/5oz/generous ½ cup soft light
   brown sugar
seeds of 1 vanilla pod (bean)
1 egg
350g/12oz/3 cups plain
   (all-purpose) flour
7.5ml/1½ tsp bicarbonate of soda
   (baking soda)
5ml/1 tsp salt
150ml/¼ pint/⅔ cup buttermilk

For the filling
200ml/7fl oz/scant 1 cup double
   (heavy) cream
40g/1½oz/3 tbsp caster
   (superfine) sugar
finely grated rind and juice of
   ½ lemon
5ml/1 tsp lemon extract

For the icing and decoration
150g/5oz/1¼ cups icing
   (confectioners') sugar
25ml/1½ tbsp lemon juice
finely grated rind of 1 lemon

1 Preheat the oven to 180°C/350°F/
Gas 4. Line two baking trays with
baking parchment or silicone mats.

2 To make the cakes, place the teabag
and boiling water in a cup. Set aside.
Beat the butter, sugar and vanilla
seeds together until light and fluffy.
Beat in the egg.

3 In a separate bowl, sift the flour
with the bicarbonate of soda and
salt. Fold half of the dry ingredients
into the butter mixture. Mix in the
buttermilk, then the remainder of
the dry ingredients.

4 Squeeze the teabag and discard.
Fold the Earl Grey tea into the cake
mixture (batter).

5 Using a piping (pastry) bag fitted
with a large plain nozzle, pipe 12
5cm/2in rounds of cake mixture 5cm/
2in apart on each of the baking trays.
Bake for 12–15 minutes, or until the
cakes bounce back when pressed.
Transfer to a wire rack to cool.

6 For the filling, whip the cream and
sugar until stiff peaks form. Fold in
the lemon rind and juice, and lemon
extract. Mix the icing sugar and
lemon juice to form a smooth icing.

7 Using a piping bag fitted with a
star-shaped nozzle, pipe some filling
on to the flat side of one cake and top
with the flat side of another. Repeat to
make 12 pies. Drizzle the tops with
icing. Decorate with lemon rind.

Nutritional information: Energy 383kcal/1612kJ; Protein 4g; Carbohydrate 53g, of which sugars 31g; Fat 19g, of which saturates 12g; Cholesterol 68mg; Calcium 76mg; Fibre 1.1g; Sodium 326mg.

Jasmine passion whoopie pies

A floral-scented whoopie pie, this unusual treat combines the flavours of jasmine extract, passion fruit and orange flower water. These look beautiful when decorated with some jasmine flowers, although they are pretty enough without, if you cannot get hold of them.

MAKES 12 WHOOPIE PIES

For the cakes
130g/4½oz/generous ½ cup
 unsalted butter, softened
150g/5oz/¾ cup caster
 (superfine) sugar
seeds of 1 vanilla pod (bean)
1 egg
325g/11½oz/scant 3 cups plain
 (all-purpose) flour
7.5ml/1½ tsp bicarbonate of soda
 (baking soda)
5ml/1 tsp salt
150ml/¼ pint/⅔ cup buttermilk
5ml/1 tsp jasmine extract
juice of 1 passion fruit
5ml/1 tsp orange flower water

For the buttercream filling
300g/11oz/2¾ cups icing
 (confectioners') sugar
seeds of 1 vanilla pod (bean)
150g/5oz/10 tbsp unsalted
 butter, softened
90ml/6 tbsp double (heavy) cream

For the glaze and decoration
90ml/6 tbsp icing
 (confectioners') sugar
juice of 2 passion fruits
white sprinkles and jasmine
 flowers, to decorate

1 Preheat the oven to 180°C/350°F/ Gas 4. Line two baking trays with baking parchment or silicone mats.

2 For the cakes, whisk the butter, sugar and vanilla seeds together until light and fluffy. Whisk in the egg.

3 In a separate bowl, sift the flour with the bicarbonate of soda and salt. In a measuring jug (cup), mix the buttermilk, jasmine extract, passion fruit juice and orange flower water.

4 Fold half of the dry ingredients into the butter mixture. Mix in the buttermilk mixture, then add the remainder of the dry ingredients and mix until fully incorporated.

5 Using a piping (pastry) bag fitted with a large plain nozzle, pipe 12 5cm/2in rounds of cake mixture (batter) 5cm/2in apart on each baking tray. Bake for 12–15 minutes, or until the cakes bounce back when gently pressed. Transfer to a wire rack and leave to cool.

6 For the filling, place the icing sugar, vanilla seeds and butter in a bowl. Using an electric whisk on medium speed, whisk the ingredients together until lightly crumbly. Slowly whisk in the cream, then turn the speed to high and whisk until creamy and smooth. Mix the icing sugar and passion fruit juice together to form a smooth glaze.

7 Using a piping bag fitted with a star-shaped nozzle, pipe some filling on to the flat side of one cake and top with the flat side of another. Repeat to make 12 pies. Spread the tops of the pies with the glaze and decorate with sprinkles and jasmine flowers.

Nutritional information: Energy 496kcal/2095kJ; Protein 4g; Carbohydrate 70g, of which sugars 49g; Fat 24g, of which saturates 15g; Cholesterol 84mg; Calcium 70mg; Fibre 1.0g; Sodium 327mg.

Cardamom and clove whoopie pies

Ground spices combine to give an earthy flavour to these delicious whoopies. The spice flavours infuse even more a few days after baking…if you can wait that long to try one! These whoopies are given a fun 'butterfly' finish, and you could use this technique on any of the recipes in the book.

MAKES 9 WHOOPIE PIES (OR 12 WITHOUT BUTTERFLY TOPS)

For the cakes
125g/4½oz/8½ tbsp unsalted
  butter, softened
175g/6oz/¾ cup soft light
  brown sugar
seeds of 1 vanilla pod (bean)
1 egg
350g/12oz/3 cups plain
  (all-purpose) flour
7.5ml/1½ tsp bicarbonate of soda
  (baking soda)
5ml/1 tsp salt
5ml/1 tsp ground cardamom
1.5ml/¼ tsp ground cloves
250ml/8fl oz/1 cup buttermilk

For the filling
200ml/7fl oz/1 cup double
  (heavy) cream
40g/1½oz/3 tbsp caster
  (superfine) sugar
2.5ml/½ tsp ground cardamom
0.75ml/⅛ tsp ground cloves

icing (confectioners') sugar and
  ground cinnamon, for sprinkling

1 Preheat the oven to 180°C/350°F/ Gas 4. Line two baking trays with baking parchment or silicone mats.

2 For the cakes, beat the butter, sugar and vanilla seeds together until light and creamy. Add the egg and beat until fully incorporated.

3 In a separate bowl, sift the flour with the bicarbonate of soda, salt, cardamom and cloves.

4 Fold half of the dry ingredients into the butter mixture. Mix in the buttermilk, then the remainder of the dry ingredients.

5 Using a piping (pastry) bag fitted with a large plain nozzle, pipe 12 5cm/2in rounds of cake mixture (batter) 5cm/2in apart on each baking tray. Bake for 12–15 minutes, or until the cakes bounce back when gently pressed. Transfer to a wire rack to cool.

6 Whip the filling ingredients together until stiff peaks form. Using a piping bag fitted with a star-shaped nozzle, pipe some filling on to the flat side of one cake and top with the flat side of another. Repeat to make 9 pies.

7 Dust the pies with icing sugar and cinnamon. There will be 6 cakes and some filling remaining. Cut 3 edges off each cake to create 18 'butterfly wings'. Discard (or eat!) the triangles in the centre. Put a spoonful of the remaining filling on each pie and arrange 2 'wings' on top. Dust with more icing sugar and cinnamon.

Nutritional information: Energy 455kcal/1911kJ; Protein 5g; Carbohydrate 56g, of which sugars 27g; Fat 25g, of which saturates 15g; Cholesterol 89mg; Calcium 119mg; Fibre 1.5g; Sodium 440mg.

Pistachio rose water whoopie pies

Light, creamy and with a subtle hint of floral extracts, these whoopie pies perfectly combine pistachios, rose water and white chocolate ganache to sumptuous ends. Try to select the prettiest pistachios you can find for the topping – those with a little pink colouring are perfect.

MAKES 12 WHOOPIE PIES

For the cakes
130g/4½oz/generous ½ cup
  unsalted butter, softened
150g/5oz/¾ cup caster
  (superfine) sugar
seeds of 1 vanilla pod (bean)
1 egg
325g/11½oz/scant 3 cups plain
  (all-purpose) flour
7.5ml/1½ tsp bicarbonate of soda
  (baking soda)
5ml/1 tsp salt
150ml/¼ pint/⅔ cup buttermilk
50ml/2fl oz/¼ cup milk
100g/3¾oz/scant 1 cup shelled
  pistachios, roughly chopped

For the ganache filling
150g/5oz white chocolate,
  chopped
40g/1½oz/3 tbsp unsalted
  butter, softened
100ml/3½fl oz/scant ½ cup double
  (heavy) cream
4 drops rose water

For the icing
150g/5oz/1¼ cups royal icing
  (confectioners') sugar
25ml/1½ tbsp cold water
1–2 drops rose water

25g/1oz/¼ cup shelled
  pistachios, roughly chopped,
  to decorate

1 Preheat the oven to 180°C/350°F/ Gas 4. Line two baking trays with baking parchment or silicone mats. For the cakes, whisk the butter, sugar and vanilla until fluffy. Whisk in the egg.

2 In a separate bowl, sift the flour with the bicarbonate of soda and salt. Fold half of the dry ingredients into the butter mixture. Mix in the buttermilk and milk, then the remainder of the dry ingredients. Fold in the pistachios.

3 Using a piping (pastry) bag fitted with a large plain nozzle, pipe 12 5cm/2in rounds of cake mixture (batter) 5cm/2in apart on each baking tray. Bake for 12–15 minutes, or until the cakes bounce back when gently pressed. Transfer to a wire rack to cool.

4 For the filling, place the chocolate and butter in a heatproof bowl. Gently heat the cream in a pan to the point just before it boils. Pour the hot cream over the chocolate and butter, add the rose water and stir until smooth.

5 Cover the bowl with clear film (plastic wrap), ensuring the clear film touches the surface of the ganache. Allow the ganache to cool at room temperature, then refrigerate for 30 minutes–1 hour, until thickened.

6 Mix the icing ingredients together to form a smooth, thick paste. Place a tablespoonful of ganache on to the flat side of one cake and top with the flat side of another. Repeat to make 12 pies. Spread icing over the tops and sprinkle with chopped pistachios.

Nutritional information: Energy 480kcal/2019kJ; Protein 7g; Carbohydrate 56g, of which sugars 35g; Fat 27g, of which saturates 14g; Cholesterol 64mg; Calcium 114mg; Fibre 1.0g; Sodium 392mg.

Lavender coconut whoopie pies

Pretty and purple, these whoopie pies are a delight for the eye as well as the tastebuds. The coconut milk lends itself perfectly as a carrier for the lavender oils. You can make lavender oil at home by putting edible lavender flowers in a bottle of light olive oil and leaving to infuse for 1 month.

MAKES 12 WHOOPIE PIES

For the cakes
150g/5oz/10 tbsp unsalted
  butter, softened
150g/5oz/generous ½ cup soft light
  brown sugar
50g/2oz/¼ cup caster
  (superfine) sugar
seeds of 1 vanilla pod (bean)
2 eggs
350g/12oz/3 cups plain
  (all-purpose) flour
7.5ml/1½ tsp bicarbonate of soda
  (baking soda)
5ml/1 tsp salt
150ml/¼ pint/⅔ cup coconut milk
3–4 drops edible lavender oil

For the filling
500ml/17fl oz/generous 2 cups
  double (heavy) cream
30ml/2 tbsp lavender honey

For the icing
150g/5oz/1¼ cups icing
  (confectioners') sugar
25ml/1½ tbsp cold water
5–10ml/1–2 tsp lavender
  food colouring
1–2 drops lavender extract

For the decoration
20g/¾oz fresh lavender flowers

1 Preheat the oven to 180°C/350°F/ Gas 4. Line two baking trays with baking parchment or silicone mats.

2 For the cakes, whisk the butter, sugars and vanilla seeds together. Whisk in the eggs, one at a time.

3 In a separate bowl, sift the flour with the bicarbonate of soda and salt. In a measuring jug (cup), stir the coconut milk and lavender oil together. Fold half of the dry ingredients into the butter mixture. Mix in the coconut milk mixture, then mix in the remainder of the dry ingredients.

4 Using a piping (pastry) bag fitted with a large plain nozzle, pipe 12 5cm/ 2in rounds of cake mixture (batter) 5cm/2in apart on each baking tray.

5 Bake for 12–15 minutes, or until the cakes bounce back when gently pressed. Transfer to a wire rack to cool. For the filling, whip the cream until stiff peaks form. Fold in the honey.

6 Mix the icing ingredients together to form a smooth paste.

7 Using a piping bag fitted with a star-shaped nozzle, pipe some filling on to the flat side of one cake and top with the flat side of another. Repeat to make 12 pies. Spread icing over the tops and decorate with lavender flowers.

Nutritional information: Energy 543kcal/2274kJ; Protein 5g; Carbohydrate 58g, of which sugars 36g; Fat 34g, of which saturates 21g; Cholesterol 126mg; Calcium 80mg; Fibre 1.1g; Sodium 346mg.

Ginger lychee whoopie pies

The fiery heat of ginger is counterbalanced by the cool sweetness of plump and juicy lychees in this tasty recipe. They are best assembled just before serving, but you can always make the cakes in advance and store them in an airtight container until you are ready to fill them and serve.

MAKES 12 WHOOPIE PIES

For the cakes
130g/4½oz/generous ½ cup
  unsalted butter, softened
150g/5oz/generous ½ cup soft light
  brown sugar
seeds of 1 vanilla pod (bean)
1 egg
350g/12oz/3 cups plain
  (all-purpose) flour
7.5ml/1½ tsp bicarbonate of soda
  (baking soda)
5ml/1 tsp salt
5ml/1 tsp ground ginger
150ml/¼ pint/⅔ cup buttermilk
50ml/2fl oz/¼ cup milk
75g/3oz crystallized (candied)
  preserved stem ginger,
  finely chopped

For the filling
2 egg whites
130g/4½oz/scant ¾ cup caster
  (superfine) sugar
225g/8oz/1 cup unsalted
  butter, softened
10 fresh lychees, peeled, stoned
  (pitted) and finely chopped
2.5ml/½ tsp ground ginger

For the icing and decoration
150g/5oz/1¼ cups icing
  (confectioners') sugar
25ml/1½ tbsp cold water
5–10ml/1–2 tsp pink food colouring
pink sprinkles, to decorate

1 Preheat the oven to 180°C/350°F/
Gas 4. Line two baking trays with
baking parchment or silicone mats.

2 For the cakes, whisk the butter,
sugar and vanilla seeds together until
light and fluffy. Whisk in the egg. In
a separate bowl, sift the flour with
the bicarbonate of soda, salt and
ground ginger. Fold half of the dry
ingredients into the butter mixture.
Mix in the buttermilk and milk, then
the remainder of the dry ingredients.
Fold in the crystallized ginger.

3 Using a piping (pastry) bag fitted
with a large plain nozzle, pipe 12 5cm/
2in rounds of cake mixture (batter)
5cm/2in apart on each baking tray.
Bake for 12–15 minutes, or until the
cakes bounce back when gently
pressed. Transfer to a wire rack to cool.

4 For the filling, put the egg whites
and sugar in a heatproof bowl set over
a pan of simmering water. Using an
electric whisk, whisk until the sugar
has dissolved and the mixture turns
white and hot. Remove from the heat
and whisk on high speed until the
bottom of the bowl starts to cool.
Turn the speed to low and whisk in
the butter, a little at a time. Fold in the
lychees and ground ginger. Chill for
30 minutes–1 hour, until thickened.

5 For the icing, mix the icing sugar,
water and food colouring together to
form a smooth, thick paste.

6 Using a piping bag fitted with a
star-shaped nozzle, pipe some filling
on to the flat side of one cake and top
with the flat side of another. Repeat to
make 12 pies. Spread icing over the
tops and decorate with sprinkles.

Nutritional information: Energy 327kcal/1384kJ; Protein 5g; Carbohydrate 57g, of which sugars 37g; Fat 11g, of which saturates 7g; Cholesterol 45mg; Calcium 78mg; Fibre 0.9g; Sodium 379mg.

Sour strawberry whoopie pies

Fresh strawberries combine with the sweet and sour tang of lemon curd in these summery whoopie pies. There will be extra lemon curd left over, which you can store in an airtight container in the refrigerator for 2–3 weeks. You could always use store-bought lemon curd, if time is short.

MAKES 12 WHOOPIE PIES

For the cakes
150g/5oz/10 tbsp unsalted
    butter, softened
150g/5oz/generous ½ cup soft light
    brown sugar
50g/2oz/¼ cup caster
    (superfine) sugar
seeds of 1 vanilla pod (bean)
2 eggs
350g/12oz/3 cups plain
    (all-purpose) flour
7.5ml/1½ tsp bicarbonate of soda
    (baking soda)
5ml/1 tsp salt
150ml/¼ pint/⅔ cup buttermilk

**For the lemon curd and
    strawberry filling**
3 eggs
finely grated rind and juice of
    3 lemons
200g/7oz/1 cup caster
    (superfine) sugar
100g/3¾oz/scant ½ cup unsalted
    butter, diced
150g/5oz/1 cup fresh strawberries,
    hulled and chopped

For the icing and decoration
150g/5oz/1¼ cups icing
    (confectioners') sugar
25ml/1½ tbsp fresh strawberry juice
3–4 strawberries, sliced, to decorate

1 Preheat the oven to 180°C/350°F/ Gas 4. Line two baking trays with baking parchment or silicone mats. For the cakes, whisk the butter, sugars and vanilla seeds until light and creamy. Whisk in the eggs, one at a time.

2 In a separate bowl, sift the flour with the bicarbonate of soda and salt. Fold half of the dry ingredients into the butter mixture. Mix in the buttermilk, then the rest of the dry ingredients.

3 Using a piping (pastry) bag fitted with a large plain nozzle, pipe 12 5cm/2in rounds of cake mixture (batter) 5cm/2in apart on each baking tray. Bake for 12–15 minutes, or until the cakes bounce back when gently pressed. Transfer to a wire rack to cool.

4 To make the lemon curd, put the eggs, lemon rind and juice, sugar and butter in a heatproof bowl set over a pan of simmering water. Whisk together over low heat for 10 minutes, or until the mixture thickens. Do not allow the mixture to boil or overheat, otherwise it will curdle. Remove from the heat, leave to cool, then cover with clear film (plastic wrap) and refrigerate until thickened.

5 Take about 300g/11oz of the lemon curd and fold in the strawberries. The remaining lemon curd can be stored in the refrigerator for future use.

6 To make the icing, mix the icing sugar and strawberry juice together in a small bowl to form a smooth paste.

7 Place a tablespoonful of strawberry lemon curd on to the flat side of one cake and top with the flat side of another. Repeat to make 12 pies. Spread icing over the top of each pie and decorate with sliced strawberries.

Nutritional information: Energy 478kcal/2022kJ; Protein 7g; Carbohydrate 72g, of which sugars 50g; Fat 20g, of which saturates 12g; Cholesterol 147mg; Calcium 86mg; Fibre 1.4g; Sodium 354mg.

Chocolate and chilli whoopie pies

Chocolate and chilli marry together to create a winning combination in these whoopie pies. You can alter the amount of chilli powder you put in the filling to suit your own taste. For the more adventurous, try adding 1 finely chopped and seeded fresh red chilli to the cake mixture.

2 In a separate bowl, sift the flour with the cocoa powder, bicarbonate of soda, cayenne and salt. Fold half of the dry ingredients into the butter mixture. Mix in the buttermilk and milk, then the rest of the dry ingredients.

3 Using a piping (pastry) bag fitted with a large plain nozzle, pipe 12 5cm/2in rounds of cake mixture (batter) 5cm/2in apart on each baking tray. Bake for 12–15 minutes, or until the cakes bounce back when gently pressed. Transfer to a wire rack to cool.

4 For the filling, place the chocolate, butter and cream in a heatproof bowl set over a pan of simmering water. Heat gently, stirring occasionally, until melted and smooth. Stir in the chilli powder, then remove the bowl, dry the base and cover with clear film (plastic wrap), ensuring it touches the surface of the ganache. Allow to cool, then refrigerate for 30 minutes–1 hour, until thickened.

MAKES 12 WHOOPIE PIES

For the cakes
130g/4½oz/generous ½ cup
  unsalted butter, softened
150g/5oz/¾ cup caster
  (superfine) sugar
seeds of 1 vanilla pod (bean)
1 egg
350g/12oz/3 cups plain
  (all-purpose) flour
40g/1½oz unsweetened cocoa
  powder
7.5ml/1½ tsp bicarbonate of soda
  (baking soda)
5ml/1 tsp cayenne pepper
5ml/1 tsp salt
150ml/¼ pint/⅔ cup buttermilk
50ml/2fl oz/¼ cup milk

For the ganache filling
150g/5oz dark (bittersweet)
  chocolate, chopped
40g/1½oz/3 tbsp unsalted
  butter, softened
100ml/3½fl oz/scant ½ cup double
  (heavy) cream
5ml/1 tsp chilli powder

For the topping
100g/3¾oz dark (bittersweet)
  chocolate, melted
15ml/1 tbsp dried chilli flakes

1 Preheat the oven to 180°C/350°F/Gas 4. Line two baking trays with baking parchment or silicone mats. For the cakes, whisk the butter, sugar and vanilla until fluffy. Whisk in the egg.

5 Using a piping bag fitted with a star-shaped nozzle, pipe some ganache on to the flat side of one cake and top with the flat side of another. Repeat to make 12 pies. Drizzle a little melted chocolate on the tops. Sprinkle with chilli flakes.

Nutritional information: Energy 383kcal/1609kJ; Protein 6g; Carbohydrate 39g, of which sugars 16g; Fat 24g, of which saturates 15g; Cholesterol 66mg; Calcium 83mg; Fibre 1.3g; Sodium 357mg.

Pepper and pear whoopie pies

Spicy and sweet, with plenty of white, black and pink peppercorns and pieces of fresh juicy pear, the contrasting flavours of these whoopie pies work perfectly together. You could try the same recipe with ripe peaches or soft summer berries, for an interesting change.

MAKES 12 WHOOPIE PIES

For the cakes
150g/5oz/10 tbsp unsalted
    butter, softened
150g/5oz/generous ½ cup soft light
    brown sugar
50g/2oz/¼ cup caster (superfine) sugar
seeds of 1 vanilla pod (bean)
2 eggs
350g/12oz/3 cups plain
    (all-purpose) flour
7.5ml/1½ tsp bicarbonate of soda
    (baking soda)
5ml/1 tsp salt
2.5ml/½ tsp ground white pepper
2.5ml/½ tsp ground pink peppercorns
2.5ml/½ tsp ground black pepper
150ml/¼ pint/⅔ cup buttermilk

For the filling
2 egg whites
130g/4½oz/scant ¾ cup caster
    (superfine) sugar
seeds of 1 vanilla pod (bean)
225g/8oz/1 cup unsalted
    butter, softened
2 pears, peeled, cored and
    finely chopped

For the icing and decoration
150g/5oz/1¼ cups icing
    (confectioners') sugar
25ml/1½ tbsp cold water
25g/1oz/¼ cup shelled pistachios,
    roughly chopped

1 Preheat the oven to 180°C/350°F/ Gas 4. Line two baking trays with baking parchment or silicone mats. For the cakes, whisk the butter, sugars and vanilla until fluffy. Whisk in the eggs.

2 In a separate bowl, sift the flour with the bicarbonate of soda, salt and ground peppers. Fold half of the dry ingredients into the butter mixture. Mix in the buttermilk, then the remainder of the dry ingredients.

3 Using a piping (pastry) bag fitted with a large plain nozzle, pipe 12 5cm/2in rounds of cake mixture (batter) 5cm/2in apart on each baking tray. Bake for 12–15 minutes, or until the cakes bounce back when pressed. Transfer to a wire rack to cool.

4 For the filling, put the egg whites, sugar and vanilla in a heatproof bowl set over a pan of simmering water. Using an electric whisk, whisk until the sugar has dissolved and the mixture is white and hot. Remove from the heat and whisk on high speed until the bottom of the bowl starts to cool. Turn the speed to low and whisk in the butter, a little at a time. Gently fold in the chopped pears.

5 To make the icing, mix the icing sugar and water together in a small bowl to form a smooth, thick paste.

6 To assemble the pies, place a tablespoonful of filling on to the flat side of one cake and top with the flat side of another. Repeat with the remaining cakes and filling to make 12 pies. Spread a little icing on top of each whoopie pie and sprinkle with chopped pistachios.

Nutritional information: Energy 537kcal/2267kJ; Protein 6g; Carbohydrate 69g, of which sugars 47g; Fat 29g, of which saturates 17g; Cholesterol 112mg; Calcium 81mg; Fibre 1.1g; Sodium 354mg.

Pink peppercorn and peanut whoopie pies

Peanuts and milk chocolate are a great combination, and these whoopie pies offer an extra dimension by adding some fiery pink peppercorns to the mix. The cakes are lovely served hot from the oven, spread with the ganache and sprinkled with chopped peanuts.

MAKES 12 WHOOPIE PIES

For the cakes
130g/4½oz/generous ½ cup unsalted
  butter, softened
150g/5oz/¾ cup caster
  (superfine) sugar
seeds of 1 vanilla pod (bean)
1 egg
325g/11½oz/scant 3 cups plain
  (all-purpose) flour
7.5ml/1½ tsp bicarbonate of soda
  (baking soda)
5ml/1 tsp salt
150ml/¼ pint/⅔ cup buttermilk
50ml/2fl oz/¼ cup milk
100g/3¾oz/scant 1 cup dry roasted
  salted peanuts, chopped
5ml/1 tsp ground pink peppercorns

For the ganache filling
150g/5oz dark (bittersweet) chocolate
40g/1½oz/3 tbsp unsalted
  butter, softened
100ml/3½fl oz/scant ½ cup double
  (heavy) cream

For the topping and decoration
100g/3¾oz milk chocolate, melted
25g/1oz/¼ cup dry roasted salted
  peanuts, chopped
12 dry roasted salted peanut halves

1 Preheat the oven to 180°C/350°F/Gas 4. Line two baking trays with baking parchment or silicone mats. For the cakes, whisk the butter, sugar and vanilla until light and fluffy. Whisk in the egg.

2 In a separate bowl, sift the flour with the bicarbonate of soda and salt. Fold half of the dry ingredients into the butter mixture. Mix in the buttermilk and milk, then the remaining dry ingredients. Stir in the nuts and pepper.

3 Using an ice cream scoop, scoop 12 5cm/2in rounds of cake mixture (batter) 5cm/2in apart on each baking tray. Bake for 12–15 minutes, or until the cakes bounce back when gently pressed. Transfer to a wire rack to cool.

4 For the filling, break the chocolate up and place it, along with the butter and cream, in a heatproof bowl set over a pan of simmering water. Heat gently, stirring, until melted and smooth. Remove the bowl from the pan, dry the base, then cover it with clear film (plastic wrap), ensuring it touches the surface of the ganache. Allow to cool, then refrigerate for 30 minutes–1 hour, until thickened.

5 Place a tablespoonful of filling on to the flat side of one cake and top with the flat side of another. Repeat to make 12 pies. Roll the edges in chopped nuts. Spread melted chocolate on the tops, and top each with a peanut half.

Nutritional information: Energy 475kcal/1991kJ; Protein 8g; Carbohydrate 48g, of which sugars 27g; Fat 29g, of which saturates 15g; Cholesterol 69mg; Calcium 120mg; Fibre 1.8g; Sodium 425mg.

Cola cake whoopie pies

The fizzy cola drink in these whoopie pie cakes gives a lovely lightness to the pies and the vanilla intensifies the sweet cola flavour. If you want to achieve a deeper cola flavour, try adding a few drops of cola extract to the cake mixture. These are great cakes to serve at children's parties.

MAKES 12 WHOOPIE PIES

For the cakes
130g/4½oz/generous ½ cup unsalted
   butter, softened
150g/5oz/¾ cup caster
   (superfine) sugar
seeds of 1 vanilla pod (bean)
1 egg
325g/11½oz/scant 3 cups plain
   (all-purpose) flour
7.5ml/1½ tsp bicarbonate of soda
   (baking soda)
5ml/1 tsp salt
150ml/¼ pint/⅔ cup cola soft drink

For the buttercream filling
300g/11oz/2¾ cups icing
   (confectioners') sugar
seeds of 1 vanilla pod (bean)
150g/5oz/10 tbsp unsalted
   butter, softened
90ml/6 tbsp double (heavy) cream

For the icing and decoration
150g/5oz/1¼ cups icing
   (confectioners') sugar
25ml/1½ tbsp cola soft drink
50g/2oz cola-flavoured hard-boiled
   sweets (candies), crushed
cola bottle sweets, to decorate

1 Preheat the oven to 180°C/350°F/ Gas 4. Line two baking trays with baking parchment or silicone mats.

2 For the cakes, beat the butter, sugar and vanilla seeds until light and creamy. Beat in the egg. In a separate bowl, sift the flour with the bicarbonate of soda and salt. Fold half of the dry ingredients into the butter mixture.

3 Mix in the cola, then mix in the remainder of the dry ingredients.

4 Using a piping (pastry) bag fitted with a large plain nozzle, pipe 12 5cm/ 2in rounds of cake mixture (batter) 5cm/2in apart on each baking tray. Bake for 12–15 minutes, or until the cakes bounce back when gently pressed. Transfer to a wire rack to cool.

5 For the filling, place the icing sugar, vanilla seeds and butter in a bowl. Using an electric whisk on medium speed, whisk together until lightly crumbly. Slowly whisk in the cream, then increase the speed to high and whisk until the mixture is smooth.

6 For the icing, mix the icing sugar and cola together to form a smooth paste.

7 Using a piping bag fitted with a tiny nozzle, pipe a thin line of filling around the edge of each cake. Roll in crushed cola sweets. Using a small plain nozzle, pipe some filling on to the flat side of one cake and top with the flat side of another. Repeat to make 12 pies. Spread a little icing over the tops of the pies and top with cola bottles.

Nutritional information: Energy 529kcal/2237kJ; Protein 3g; Carbohydrate 79g, of which sugars 56g; Fat 24g, of which saturates 15g; Cholesterol 84mg; Calcium 51mg; Fibre 1.0g; Sodium 321mg.

Cream soda whoopie pies

The cream soda in these whoopie pies provides the cakes with extra lift, making them lighter and fluffier than buttermilk whoopie pies. The blueberries give a tart, fresh kick to the sweet marshmallow filling and the baby blue icing makes them picture perfect!

4 Bake for 12–15 minutes, or until the cakes bounce back when pressed. Transfer to a wire rack to cool.

5 To make the marshmallow, place the boiling water in the bowl of an electric mixer and sprinkle with the gelatine. Whisk on low speed until the gelatine dissolves. Set aside.

6 In a deep pan, heat the sugar, golden syrup and cold water until the mixture comes to a rolling boil. With the electric mixer on low, gradually pour the hot sugar syrup into the bowl containing the gelatine mixture. Turn the mixer up to high speed and whisk for 5 minutes or until it is very thick, pale and fluffy. Fold in the blueberries.

7 For the icing, mix the icing sugar, cream soda and food colouring together to form a smooth paste.

8 Using two oiled tablespoons, place a spoonful of filling on to the flat side of one cake and top with the flat side of another. Repeat to make 12 pies. Spread a little icing over the tops of the pies and decorate each with a blueberry.

MAKES 12 WHOOPIE PIES

For the cakes
150g/5oz/10 tbsp unsalted
  butter, softened
150g/5oz/generous ½ cup soft light
  brown sugar
seeds of 1 vanilla pod (bean)
1 egg
350g/12oz/3 cups plain
  (all-purpose) flour
7.5ml/1½ tsp bicarbonate of soda
  (baking soda)
5ml/1 tsp salt
150ml/¼ pint/⅔ cup cream soda

For the marshmallow filling
50ml/2fl oz/¼ cup boiling water
15ml/1 tbsp powdered gelatine
175g/6oz/generous ¾ cup caster
  (superfine) sugar
75ml/2½fl oz/⅓ cup golden
  (light corn) syrup
25ml/1½ tbsp cold water
150g/5oz/1¼ cups fresh blueberries

For the icing and decoration
150g/5oz/1¼ cups icing
  (confectioners') sugar
25ml/1½ tbsp cream soda
1–2 tsp blue food colouring
12 blueberries

1 Preheat the oven to 180°C/350°F/ Gas 4. Line two baking trays with baking parchment or silicone mats.

2 For the cakes, beat the butter, sugar and vanilla seeds until creamy. Beat in the egg. In a separate bowl, sift the flour with the bicarbonate of soda and salt. Fold half of the dry ingredients into the butter mixture. Mix in the cream soda, then the rest of the dry ingredients.

3 Using a piping (pastry) bag fitted with a large plain nozzle, pipe 12 5cm/2in rounds of cake mixture (batter) 5cm/2in apart on each baking tray.

Nutritional information: Energy 385kcal/1631kJ; Protein 4g; Carbohydrate 72g, of which sugars 47g; Fat 11g, of which saturates 7g; Cholesterol 49mg; Calcium 67mg; Fibre 2.2g; Sodium 338mg.

Liquorice delight whoopie pies

These striking, black whoopie pies are made using ground aniseed and filled with contrasting white marshmallow. They are perfect for all liquorice lovers, who are sure to nibble the liquorice sweet from the top before they take their first bite!

MAKES 12 WHOOPIE PIES

For the cakes
125g/4¼oz/8½ tbsp unsalted
   butter, softened
175g/6oz/¾ cup soft light
   brown sugar
seeds of 1 vanilla pod (bean)
1 egg
350g/12oz/3 cups plain
   (all-purpose) flour
7.5ml/1½ tsp bicarbonate of soda
   (baking soda)
5ml/1 tsp salt
10ml/2 tsp ground aniseed
250ml/8fl oz/1 cup buttermilk
5ml/1 tsp black food colouring

For the marshmallow filling
50ml/2fl oz/¼ cup boiling water
15ml/1 tbsp powdered gelatine
175g/6oz/generous ¾ cup caster
   (superfine) sugar
75ml/2½fl oz/⅓ cup golden
   (light corn) syrup
25ml/1½ tbsp cold water

For the icing and decoration
150g/5oz/1¼ cups icing
   (confectioners') sugar
25ml/1½ tbsp cold water
5ml/1 tsp ground aniseed
5ml/1 tsp black food colouring
purple sprinkles
12 liquorice sweets (candies)

1 Preheat the oven to 180°C/350°F/ Gas 4. Line two baking trays with baking parchment or silicone mats. For the cakes, whisk the butter, sugar and vanilla seeds together until light and creamy. Whisk in the egg.

2 In a separate bowl, sift the flour with the bicarbonate of soda, salt and ground aniseed. Fold half of the dry ingredients into the butter mixture. Mix in the buttermilk, then the rest of the dry ingredients. Stir in the colouring.

3 Using a piping (pastry) bag fitted with a large plain nozzle, pipe 12 5cm/ 2in rounds of cake mixture (batter) 5cm/2in apart on each baking tray. Bake for 12–15 minutes, or until the cakes bounce back when gently pressed. Transfer to a wire rack to cool.

4 To make the marshmallow, place the boiling water in the bowl of an electric mixer and sprinkle with the gelatine. Whisk on low speed until the gelatine dissolves. Set aside. In a deep pan, heat the sugar, golden syrup and cold water until it comes to a rolling boil, stirring. With the electric mixer on low, gradually pour the hot sugar syrup into the mixing bowl. Turn the mixer to high and whisk for 5 minutes or until thick, pale and fluffy.

5 For the icing, mix the icing sugar, water, ground aniseed and colouring together to form a paste. Place a tablespoonful of filling on to the flat side of one cake and top with the flat side of another. Repeat to make 12 pies. Roll the edge of the filling in sprinkles. Spread icing over the top of each pie and top with a liquorice sweet.

Nutritional information: Energy 390kcal/1656kJ; Protein 5g; Carbohydrate 76g, of which sugars 52g; Fat 10g, of which saturates 6g; Cholesterol 44mg; Calcium 113mg; Fibre 1.1g; Sodium 359mg.

Holiday and special occasion whoopies

Covering a medley of events, these whoopie pies capture the holiday spirit and the heart of special occasions. Birthdays, weddings, Easter, Halloween and Christmas are all covered in this chapter with fun, festive and elegant recipes. Of course, you don't have to make these only on special occasions. The Valentine's Day Whoopie Pies will be just as delicious, with their classic strawberry and cream filling, when served as normal round whoopies. Or even surprise your loved one with a heart-shaped whoopie at any time of year!

Sesame and red bean whoopie pies

These fun whoopies are a great way to celebrate Chinese New Year. You can enhance the flavour of the sesame seeds by toasting them lightly before adding them to the cake mixture. The sesame cakes are sandwiched with a sweet red bean paste that isn't widely available, but is very easy to make.

MAKES 12 WHOOPIE PIES

For the cakes
130g/4½oz/generous ½ cup unsalted butter, softened
150g/5oz/¾ cup caster (superfine) sugar
seeds of 1 vanilla pod (bean)
1 egg
325g/11½oz/scant 3 cups plain (all-purpose) flour
7.5ml/1½ tsp bicarbonate of soda (baking soda)
5ml/1 tsp salt
50ml/2fl oz/¼ cup milk
150ml/¼ pint/⅔ cup buttermilk
100g/3¾oz/½ cup sesame seeds

For the filling
400g/14oz canned drained red aduki beans, rinsed
75g/3oz/6 tbsp caster (superfine) sugar
75ml/5 tbsp double (heavy) cream
15ml/1 tbsp sesame oil

For the icing and decoration
150g/5oz/1¼ cups icing (confectioners') sugar
25ml/1½ tbsp fresh orange juice
25g/1oz/2 tbsp sesame seeds

1 Preheat the oven to 180°C/350°F/ Gas 4. Line two baking trays with baking parchment or silicone mats.

2 For the cakes, whisk the butter, sugar and vanilla until creamy. Whisk in the egg. In a separate bowl, sift the flour with the bicarbonate of soda and salt.

3 Fold half of the dry ingredients into the butter mixture. Mix in the milk and buttermilk, then the remaining dry ingredients. Mix in the sesame seeds.

4 Using a piping (pastry) bag fitted with a large plain nozzle, pipe 12 5cm/2in rounds of cake mixture (batter) 5cm/2in apart on each baking tray. Bake for 12–15 minutes, or until golden. Transfer to a wire rack to cool.

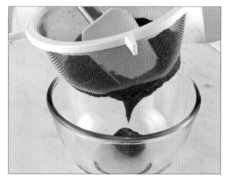

5 For the filling, mash the beans in a bowl or process in a blender until smooth. Press the mashed or blended beans through a sieve (strainer) into a bowl. Discard the skins left in the sieve. Add the sugar, cream and sesame oil to the bean purée. Mix well.

6 For the icing, mix the icing sugar and orange juice to form a paste. Place a tablespoonful of the red bean filling on to the flat side of one cake and top with the flat side of another. Repeat to make 12 pies. Spread icing on the tops and sprinkle with sesame seeds.

Nutritional information: Energy 444kcal/1873kJ; Protein 8g; Carbohydrate 60g, of which sugars 34g; Fat 21g, of which saturates 9g; Cholesterol 54mg; Calcium 147mg; Fibre 01.0g; Sodium 325mg.

Valentine's Day whoopie pies

Romance was never easier to create than with these heart-shaped whoopie pies, made with the classic combination of strawberries and cream. You can also bake the cake mixture all together in a Swiss roll tin (jelly roll pan), then cut out the heart shapes using a pastry cutter.

MAKES 12 WHOOPIE PIES

For the cakes
125g/4¼oz/8½ tbsp unsalted
   butter, softened
175g/6oz/¾ cup soft light
   brown sugar
seeds of 1 vanilla pod (bean)
1 egg
350g/12oz/3 cups plain
   (all-purpose) flour
7.5ml/1½ tsp bicarbonate of soda
   (baking soda)
5ml/1 tsp salt
250ml/8fl oz/1 cup buttermilk

For the filling
250ml/8fl oz/1 cup whipping cream
40g/1½oz/3 tbsp caster
   (superfine) sugar
seeds of 1 vanilla pod (bean)
75g/3oz/½ cup strawberries, hulled
   and chopped

For the icing and decoration
150g/5oz/1¼ cups icing
   (confectioners') sugar
25ml/1½ tbsp lemon juice
2–3 strawberries, hulled and sliced

1 Preheat the oven to 180°C/350°F/ Gas 4. Line two baking trays with baking parchment or silicone mats.

2 To make the cakes, beat the butter, sugar and vanilla seeds together until light and creamy. Beat in the egg.

3 In a separate bowl, sift the flour with the bicarbonate of soda and salt. Fold half of the dry ingredients into the butter mixture.

4 Mix in the buttermilk, then add the remainder of the dry ingredients and mix until fully incorporated.

5 Using a piping (pastry) bag fitted with a large plain nozzle, pipe 12 5cm/2in rounds of cake mixture (batter) 5cm/2in apart on each baking tray. Bake for 12–15 minutes, or until the cakes bounce back when gently pressed. Transfer to a wire rack to cool.

6 For the filling, whip the cream until soft peaks form. Whisk in the sugar and vanilla seeds, then fold in the chopped strawberries.

7 For the icing, mix the icing sugar and lemon juice to form a paste.

8 Using a small heart-shaped pastry (cookie) cutter, cut the cakes into heart shapes.

9 Place a tablespoonful of strawberry cream filling on to the flat side of one cake and top with the flat side of another. Repeat to make 12 pies. Spread icing over the tops and decorate each with strawberry slices.

Nutritional information: Energy 389kcal/1639kJ; Protein 5g; Carbohydrate 56g, of which sugars 34g; Fat 18g, of which saturates 11g; Cholesterol 66mg; Calcium 93mg; Fibre 1.2g; Sodium 333mg.

Hot cross bun whoopie pies

Next Easter, try a different dessert and serve these hot cross bun whoopie pies. For the decoration, cut thin strips of marzipan and arrange them in crosses on the tops of the whoopie pies. Press the marzipan strips down a little at the edges to make them stick to the cakes.

3 Stir in the rinds and dried fruit. Fold half of the flour mixture into the butter mixture. Mix in the buttermilk and milk, then the rest of the flour mixture.

4 Using a piping (pastry) bag fitted with a large plain nozzle, pipe 12 5cm/ 2in rounds of cake mixture (batter) 5cm/2in apart on each baking tray. Bake for 12–15 minutes, or until the cakes bounce back when pressed. Transfer to a wire rack to cool. Meanwhile, make the filling. Whip the cream until stiff peaks form. Whisk in the custard, sugar and vanilla seeds.

MAKES 12 WHOOPIE PIES

For the cakes
150g/5oz/10 tbsp unsalted
  butter, softened
150g/5oz/generous ½ cup soft light
  brown sugar
seeds of 1 vanilla pod (bean)
1 egg
300g/11oz/2¾ cups plain
  (all-purpose) flour
7.5ml/1½ tsp bicarbonate of soda
  (baking soda)
5ml/1 tsp salt
finely grated rind of 1 orange
finely grated rind of 1 lemon
100g/3¾oz/scant ⅔ cup mixed
  dried fruit
150ml/¼ pint/⅔ cup buttermilk
50ml/2fl oz/¼ cup milk

For the custard cream filling
120ml/4fl oz/½ cup double
  (heavy) cream
100g/3¾oz ready-made cold custard
25ml/1½ tbsp caster (superfine) sugar
seeds of 1 vanilla pod (bean)

For the decoration
50g/2oz marzipan, cut into thin strips
cinnamon, for dusting

1 Preheat the oven to 180°C/350°F/ Gas 4. Line two baking trays with baking parchment or silicone mats.

2 For the cakes, whisk the butter, sugar and vanilla together until light and fluffy. Whisk in the egg. In a separate bowl, sift the flour with the bicarbonate of soda and salt.

5 Arrange the marzipan in crosses on half of the cakes; these will be the tops. Place a tablespoon of filling on to the flat side of one plain cake and top with the flat side of a decorated cake. Repeat to make 12 pies. Dust with cinnamon.

Nutritional information: Energy 340kcal/1432kJ; Protein 4g; Carbohydrate 44g, of which sugars 25g; Fat 18g, of which saturates 10g; Cholesterol 63mg; Calcium 96mg; Fibre 1.0g; Sodium 353mg.

Mini pumpkin whoopie pies

These moist and spicy whoopie pies make perfect use of the pumpkin leftovers from the Jack-o-lanterns at Halloween. Their small size and fabulous orange icing means they are always popular with kids. Why not give them out to trick-or-treaters this Halloween?

MAKES 24 WHOOPIE PIES

For the cakes
150g/5oz/10 tbsp unsalted
   butter, softened
150g/5oz/generous ½ cup soft light
   brown sugar
seeds of 1 vanilla pod (bean)
2 eggs
325g/11½oz/scant 3 cups plain
   (all-purpose) flour
7.5ml/1½ tsp bicarbonate of soda
   (baking soda)
5ml/1 tsp salt
5ml/1 tsp ground ginger
5ml/1 tsp ground cloves
5ml/1 tsp ground cinnamon
100ml/3½fl oz/scant ½ cup buttermilk
200g/7oz cooked (or canned)
   pumpkin flesh, mashed

For the filling
2 egg whites
125g/4¼oz/generous ½ cup caster
   (superfine) sugar
225g/8oz/1 cup unsalted
   butter, softened
40g/1½oz/scant ½ cup hazelnuts,
   roughly chopped

For the icing and decoration
150g/5oz/1¼ cups icing
   (confectioners') sugar
25ml/1½ tbsp cold water
5–10ml/1–2 tsp orange food colouring
orange sprinkles, to decorate

1 Preheat the oven to 180°C/350°F/ Gas 4. Line two baking trays with baking parchment or silicone mats. For the cakes, whisk the butter, sugar and vanilla until creamy. Whisk in the eggs.

2 In a separate bowl, sift the flour with the bicarbonate of soda, salt and ground spices. Fold half of the dry ingredients into the butter mixture. Mix in the buttermilk, then the rest of the dry ingredients. Drain any liquid from the pumpkin. Fold in the flesh.

3 Using a piping (pastry) bag fitted with a large plain nozzle, pipe 24 3cm/1¼in rounds of cake mixture (batter) 4cm/1½in apart on each of the baking trays.

4 Bake for 10–12 minutes, or until the cakes bounce back when pressed. Transfer to a wire rack to cool.

5 For the filling, put the egg whites and sugar in a heatproof bowl set over a pan of simmering water. Using an electric whisk, whisk until the sugar has dissolved and the mixture is white and hot. Remove from the heat and whisk on high speed until the bottom of the bowl starts to cool. Turn the speed to low and whisk in the butter, a little at a time. Fold in the chopped hazelnuts.

6 For the icing, mix the icing sugar, water and colouring to form a paste. Place a tablespoon of filling on to the flat side of one cake and top with the flat side of another. Repeat to make 24 pies. Spread icing over the tops and decorate with sprinkles.

Nutritional information: Energy 252kcal/1061kJ; Protein 3g; Carbohydrate 30g, of which sugars 19g; Fat 15g, of which saturates 9g; Cholesterol 56mg; Calcium 4mg; Fibre 0.7g; Sodium 166mg.

Gingerbread whoopie pies

Perfect for Christmas, or in fact any time of the year, these festive whoopie pies blend together warm and comforting spices with sweet golden syrup. They look adorable with mini gingerbread man-shaped sprinkles on top, if you can get hold of them.

MAKES 24 WHOOPIE PIES

For the cakes
125g/4¼oz/8½ tbsp unsalted butter, softened
175g/6oz/¾ cup soft light brown sugar
seeds of 1 vanilla pod (bean)
1 egg
350g/12oz/3 cups plain (all-purpose) flour
7.5ml/1½ tsp bicarbonate of soda (baking soda)
5ml/1 tsp salt
5ml/1 tsp ground ginger
5ml/1 tsp ground cinnamon
1.5ml/¼ tsp ground cloves
250ml/8fl oz/1 cup buttermilk
15ml/1 tbsp golden (light corn) syrup

For the buttercream filling
300g/11oz/2¾ cups icing (confectioners') sugar
seeds of 1 vanilla pod (bean)
150g/5oz/10 tbsp unsalted butter, softened
60ml/4 tbsp double (heavy) cream
40g/1½oz unsweetened cocoa powder

For the icing and decoration
150g/5oz/1¼ cups icing (confectioners') sugar
25ml/1½ tbsp cold water
2.5ml/½ tsp ground ginger
gingerbread man-shaped sprinkles, to decorate

1 Preheat the oven to 180°C/350°F/Gas 4. Line two baking trays with baking parchment or silicone mats.

2 For the cakes, whisk the butter, sugar and vanilla until creamy. Whisk in the egg. In a separate bowl, sift the flour with the bicarbonate of soda, salt and spices. Fold half of the dry ingredients into the butter mixture. Mix in the buttermilk, then the rest of the dry ingredients. Fold in the golden syrup.

3 Using a piping (pastry) bag fitted with a large plain nozzle, pipe 24 3cm/1¼in rounds of cake mixture (batter) 4cm/1½in apart on each baking tray. Bake for 10–12 minutes, or until the cakes bounce back when gently pressed. Transfer to a wire rack to cool.

4 For the filling, whisk the icing sugar, vanilla seeds and butter, using an electric whisk on medium speed, until crumbly. Slowly whisk in the cream, then, on high speed, whisk until smooth. Fold in the cocoa powder.

5 Mix the icing sugar, water and ginger to a paste. Using a piping (pastry) bag with a small plain nozzle, pipe some filling on to the flat side of one cake and top with the flat side of another. Repeat to make 24 pies. Spread icing over the tops. Decorate with sprinkles.

Nutritional information: Energy 263kcal/1111kJ; Protein 3g; Carbohydrate 40g, of which sugars 28g; Fat 12g, of which saturates 8g; Cholesterol 40mg; Calcium 46mg; Fibre 0.6g; Sodium 184mg.

Christmas cake whoopie pies

These whoopie pies are flavoursome and festive, bursting with fruit and spices. Filled with homemade marshmallow, drizzled with brandy and topped with royal icing and red and silver balls, they embody all the joy of a Christmas cake within a few bites of whoopie pie.

MAKES 12 WHOOPIE PIES

For the cakes
125g/4¼oz/8½ tbsp unsalted
    butter, softened
175g/6oz/¾ cup soft light brown sugar
seeds of 1 vanilla pod (bean)
1 egg
300g/11oz/2¾ cups plain
    (all-purpose) flour
7.5ml/1½ tsp bicarbonate of soda
    (baking soda)
5ml/1 tsp salt
2.5ml/½ tsp ground mixed (apple
    pie) spice
2.5ml/½ tsp ground cinnamon
finely grated rind of 1 orange
finely grated rind of 1 lemon
250ml/8fl oz/1 cup buttermilk
100g/3¾oz/⅔ cup mixed dried fruit

For the marshmallow filling
50ml/2fl oz/¼ cup boiling water
15ml/1 tbsp powdered gelatine
175g/6oz/generous ¾ cup caster
    (superfine) sugar
75ml/2½fl oz/⅓ cup golden
    (light corn) syrup
25ml/1½ tbsp cold water

For the topping
100ml/3½fl oz/scant ½ cup brandy
150g/5oz/1¼ cups royal icing
    (confectioners') sugar
25ml/1½ tbsp cold water
red and silver edible balls, to decorate

1 Preheat the oven to 180°C/350°F/ Gas 4. Line two baking trays with baking parchment or silicone mats. For the cakes, whisk the butter, sugar and vanilla until fluffy. Whisk in the egg.

2 In a separate bowl, sift the flour with the bicarbonate of soda, salt and ground spices, then stir in the citrus rinds. Fold half of the dry ingredients into the butter mixture. Mix in the buttermilk, then the rest of the dry ingredients. Fold in the dried fruit.

3 Using a piping (pastry) bag fitted with a large plain nozzle, pipe 12 5cm/ 2in rounds of cake mixture (batter) 5cm/2in apart on each baking tray. Bake for 12–15 minutes, or until the cakes bounce back when gently pressed. Transfer to a wire rack to cool.

4 To make the marshmallow, place the boiling water in the bowl of an electric mixer and sprinkle with the gelatine. Whisk on low speed until the gelatine dissolves. Set aside. In a deep pan, heat the sugar, golden syrup and cold water, stirring, until it comes to a rolling boil. With the electric mixer on low, gradually pour the hot sugar syrup into the mixing bowl. Turn the mixer to high and whisk for 5 minutes or until the mixture is thick, pale and fluffy.

5 Using an oiled tablespoon, place some filling on to the flat side of one cake and top with the flat side of another. Repeat to make 12 pies. Warm the brandy then drizzle on the tops of the pies. Leave to dry while you make the icing. Mix the royal icing sugar with the water to form a thick paste. Spread the icing on the tops of the pies, using a cocktail stick (toothpick) to create the texture of snow. Decorate with red and silver balls.

Nutritional information: Energy 412kcal/1746kJ; Protein 4g; Carbohydrate 78g, of which sugars 59g; Fat 10g, of which saturates 6g; Cholesterol 44mg; Calcium 85mg; Fibre 1.7g; Sodium 350mg.

Candy cane whoopie pies

Candy cane whoopie pies are a good way to use up leftover candy canes after the holiday season. These whoopies are filled with a light marshmallow filling, which is very easy to make, but it can be replaced with store-bought marshmallow fluff. This applies to every marshmallow filling in this book.

MAKES 12 WHOOPIE PIES

For the cakes
130g/4½oz/generous ½ cup unsalted butter, softened
150g/5oz/¾ cup caster (superfine) sugar
seeds of 1 vanilla pod (bean)
1 egg
350g/12oz/3 cups plain (all-purpose) flour
7.5ml/1½ tsp bicarbonate of soda (baking soda)
5ml/1 tsp salt
150ml/¼ pint/⅔ cup buttermilk
50ml/2fl oz/¼ cup milk

For the marshmallow filling
50ml/2fl oz/¼ cup boiling water
15ml/1 tbsp powdered gelatine
175g/6oz/generous ¾ cup caster (superfine) sugar
75ml/2½fl oz/⅓ cup golden (light corn) syrup
25ml/1½ tbsp cold water

For the icing and decoration
150g/5oz/1¼ cups icing (confectioners') sugar
25ml/1½ tbsp cold water
8 candy canes, crushed
candy cane sprinkles

1 Preheat the oven to 180°C/350°F/ Gas 4. Line two baking trays with baking parchment or silicone mats. For the cakes, whisk the butter, sugar and vanilla seeds together until light and fluffy. Whisk in the egg.

2 In a separate bowl, sift the flour with the bicarbonate of soda and salt. Fold half of the dry ingredients into the butter mixture. Mix in the buttermilk and milk, then the rest of the dry ingredients. Using a piping (pastry) bag fitted with a large plain nozzle, pipe 12 5cm/2in rounds of cake mixture (batter) 5cm/2in apart on each of the lined baking trays.

3 Bake for 12–15 minutes, or until the cakes bounce back when pressed. Transfer to a wire rack to cool.

4 To make the marshmallow, place the boiling water in the bowl of an electric mixer and sprinkle with the gelatine. Whisk on low speed until the gelatine dissolves. Set aside. In a deep pan, heat the sugar, golden syrup and cold water, stirring, until the mixture comes to a rolling boil. With the mixer on low, gradually pour the hot sugar syrup into the mixing bowl containing the gelatine. Turn the mixer to high speed and whisk for 5–10 minutes or until the mixture turns very thick, pale and fluffy.

5 To make the icing, mix the icing sugar and water together in a small bowl to form a smooth, thick paste.

6 Spoon some marshmallow on to the flat side of one cake and top with the flat side of another. Repeat to make 12 pies. Roll the edges of the filling with crushed candy cane pieces. Spread a little icing over the top of each pie and decorate with candy cane sprinkles.

Nutritional information: Energy 378kcal/1603kJ; Protein 5g; Carbohydrate 72g, of which sugars 49g; Fat 10g, of which saturates 6g; Cholesterol 45mg; Calcium 71mg; Fibre 1.1g; Sodium 341mg.

Champagne and orange whoopie pies

Luscious, light and luxurious, these whoopie pies are the perfect celebratory dessert for a special occasion. Zesty and fresh tasting, they are filled with a delicious Champagne and orange ganache, making them a really decadent treat. You can try other citrus fruits instead of oranges, too.

MAKES 12 WHOOPIE PIES

For the cakes
150g/5oz/10 tbsp unsalted
    butter, softened
150g/5oz/generous ½ cup soft light
    brown sugar
50g/2oz/¼ cup caster
    (superfine) sugar
seeds of 1 vanilla pod (bean)
finely grated rind of 2 small oranges
2 eggs
350g/12oz/3 cups plain
    (all-purpose) flour
7.5ml/1½ tsp bicarbonate of soda
    (baking soda)
5ml/1 tsp salt
150ml/¼ pint/⅔ cup buttermilk
5ml/1 tsp orange flower water

For the ganache filling
150g/5oz white chocolate, chopped
40g/1½oz/3 tbsp unsalted
    butter, softened
100ml/3½fl oz/scant ½ cup double
    (heavy) cream
finely grated rind of ½ orange
5ml/1 tsp orange flower water
15–30ml/1–2 tbsp Champagne

For the orange glaze
90ml/6 tbsp icing
    (confectioners') sugar
finely grated rind and juice of
    ½ orange

1 Preheat the oven to 180°C/350°F/ Gas 4. Line two baking trays with baking parchment or silicone mats. For the cakes, whisk the butter, sugars, vanilla seeds and orange rind together until fluffy. Whisk in the eggs.

2 In a separate bowl, sift the flour with the bicarbonate of soda and salt. Fold half of the dry ingredients into the butter mixture. Mix in the buttermilk, then the rest of the dry ingredients. Mix in the orange flower water.

3 Using a piping (pastry) bag fitted with a large plain nozzle, pipe 12 5cm/ 2in rounds of cake mixture (batter) 5cm/2in apart on each baking tray. Bake for 12–15 minutes, or until the cakes bounce back when pressed. Transfer to a wire rack to cool.

4 To make the ganache, place the white chocolate, butter, cream, orange rind and orange flower water in a heatproof bowl set over a pan of simmering water. Heat gently, stirring, until the mixture is smooth. Remove the bowl from the pan, dry the base, then stir in the Champagne.

5 Cover the bowl with clear film (plastic wrap), ensuring the clear film touches the surface of the ganache. Allow to cool, then refrigerate for 30 minutes–1 hour, until thickened.

6 Mix the glaze ingredients together to form a paste. Place a tablespoonful of the ganache on to the flat side of one cake, then top with the flat side of another. Repeat to make 12 pies. Spread the glaze over the tops of the whoopie pies.

Nutritional information: Energy 438kcal/1846kJ; Protein 6g; Carbohydrate 56g, of which sugars 34g; Fat 23g, of which saturates 14g; Cholesterol 88mg; Calcium 110mg; Fibre 1.1g; Sodium 346mg.

Mini whoopie pie birthday pyramid

These chocolate whoopie pies, stacked together to form a tall whoopie pie 'cake', are bound to get children's eyes gleaming. Roll the sides of the whoopie pies in colourful rainbow sprinkles or glitter, and simply finish off with a light dusting of cocoa powder or icing sugar.

MAKES 24 WHOOPIE PIES

For the cakes
150g/5oz/10 tbsp unsalted
 butter, softened
150g/5oz/generous ½ cup soft light
 brown sugar
50g/2oz/¼ cup caster
 (superfine) sugar
seeds of 1 vanilla pod (bean)
2 eggs
350g/12oz/3 cups plain
 (all-purpose) flour
7.5ml/1½ tsp bicarbonate of soda
 (baking soda)
50g/2oz unsweetened cocoa powder
5ml/1 tsp salt
150ml/¼ pint/⅔ cup buttermilk
50ml/2fl oz/¼ cup milk

For the buttercream filling
300g/11oz/2¾ cups icing
 (confectioners') sugar
seeds of 1 vanilla pod (bean)
150g/5oz/10 tbsp unsalted
 butter, softened
90ml/6 tbsp double (heavy) cream
50g/2oz unsweetened cocoa powder

rainbow sprinkles, to decorate
icing (confectioners') sugar,
 for dusting

1 Preheat the oven to 180°C/350°F/ Gas 4. Line two baking trays with baking parchment or silicone mats. For the cakes, beat the butter, sugars and vanilla seeds together until light and creamy. Beat in the eggs, one at a time.

2 In a separate bowl, sift the flour with the bicarbonate of soda, cocoa powder and salt. Fold half of the dry ingredients into the butter mixture. Mix in the buttermilk and milk, then the rest of the dry ingredients.

3 Using a piping (pastry) bag fitted with a large plain nozzle, pipe 24 2.5cm/1in rounds of cake mixture (batter) about 2.5cm/1in apart on each baking tray. Bake for 10–12 minutes, or until the cakes bounce back when gently pressed. Transfer to a wire rack to cool.

4 To make the filling, whisk the icing sugar, vanilla seeds and butter together, using an electric whisk, until lightly crumbly. Slowly whisk in the cream, then increase the speed to high and whisk until the mixture is creamy and smooth. Fold in the cocoa powder.

5 Place a teaspoonful of buttercream on to the flat side of 24 cakes. Top with the flat sides of the remaining 24 cakes. Spread the rainbow sprinkles on a plate and roll the edges in the sprinkles to coat the buttercream. Layer the pies on a plate to form a pyramid. Dust with sifted icing sugar.

Nutritional information: Energy 265kcal/1118kJ; Protein 3g; Carbohydrate 34g, of which sugars 22g; Fat 14g, of which saturates 9g; Cholesterol 54mg; Calcium 46mg; Fibre 0.5g; Sodium 208mg.

Giant whoopie pie birthday cake

This giant chocolate whoopie pie makes a perfect birthday cake with its rich chocolate filling and domed top. This recipe produces a very moist sponge, which has an intense chocolate flavour. Alternatives to the dark chocolate topping include whipped cream or chocolate buttercream.

MAKES 1 WHOOPIE PIE CAKE
(SERVES 8–10)

For the cakes
125g/4¼oz/8½ tbsp unsalted
   butter, softened
90g/3½oz/scant ½ cup soft light
   brown sugar
90g/3½oz/½ cup caster
   (superfine) sugar
1 egg, beaten
seeds of 1 vanilla pod (bean)
300g/11oz/2¾ cups plain
   (all-purpose) flour
50g/2oz unsweetened cocoa powder
5ml/1 tsp bicarbonate of soda
   (baking soda)
5ml/1 tsp salt
250ml/8fl oz/1 cup buttermilk

For the filling
500ml/17fl oz/generous 2 cups
   double (heavy) cream
75g/3oz/6 tbsp caster
   (superfine) sugar
seeds of 1 vanilla pod (bean)
65g/2½oz unsweetened cocoa powder

For the topping
200g/7oz dark (bittersweet)
   chocolate, melted

1 Preheat the oven to 180°C/350°F/ Gas 4. Line two baking trays with baking parchment or silicone mats.

2 For the cakes, beat the butter and sugars together until light and creamy. Beat in the egg, then stir in the vanilla seeds. In a separate bowl, sift the flour with the cocoa powder, bicarbonate of soda and salt.

3 Fold half of the dry ingredients into the butter mixture. Mix the buttermilk in, then the rest of the dry ingredients.

4 Place the collar of a 24cm/9½in springform tin (pan) on to the first baking tray and spoon half of the cake mixture (batter) into the collar, spreading the cake mixture evenly. Remove the collar and repeat the process on the second baking tray. Bake for 15–20 minutes, or until the cakes bounce back when pressed. Transfer to a wire rack to cool.

5 For the filling, whip the cream with the sugar and vanilla seeds until stiff peaks form. Fold in the cocoa powder.

6 Spoon all of the filling on to the flat side of one cake to form a thick layer, spreading evenly. Gently place the other cake on top, flat side down.

7 Pour the melted chocolate over the top of the giant whoopie pie and spread it evenly with a palette knife or metal spatula, allowing it to drip down the side. Serve the cake in slices.

Nutritional information: Energy 697kcal/2915kJ; Protein 8g; Carbohydrate 66g, of which sugars 42g; Fat 46g, of which saturates 29g; Cholesterol 123mg; Calcium 130mg; Fibre 1.1g; Sodium 456mg.

Coconut and lemon whoopie wedding stack

A definite show-stopper, this wedding cake stack is assembled by arranging the whoopie pies to form an elegant pyramid. The recipe can be multiplied and made in batches depending on how many guests there are. Refrigerate the pies until just before serving to keep the buttercream thick and firm.

MAKES 24 WHOOPIE PIES

For the cakes
275g/10oz/1¼ cups unsalted
  butter, softened
275g/10oz/1¼ cups soft light
  brown sugar
seeds of 2 vanilla pods (beans)
2 eggs
600g/1lb 6oz/5½ cups plain
  (all-purpose) flour
15ml/1 tbsp bicarbonate of soda
  (baking soda)
10ml/2 tsp salt
100ml/3½fl oz/scant ½ cup milk
300ml/½ pint/1¼ cups buttermilk
200g/7oz/2⅓ cups desiccated (dry
  unsweetened shredded) coconut

For the filling
4 egg whites
250g/9oz/scant 1⅓ cups caster
  (superfine) sugar
450g/1lb/2 cups unsalted
  butter, softened
finely grated rind and juice of
  2 lemons
2.5ml/½ tsp lemon extract

For the icing and decoration
300g/11oz/2¾ cups royal icing
  (confectioners') sugar
60ml/4 tbsp lemon juice
50g/2oz/⅔ cup desiccated (dry
  unsweetened shredded) coconut
fresh pink rose petals, for sprinkling

1 Preheat the oven to 180°C/350°F/ Gas 4. Line four baking trays with baking parchment or silicone mats. For the cakes, whisk the butter, sugar and vanilla until fluffy. Whisk in the eggs.

2 In a separate bowl, sift the flour with the bicarbonate of soda and salt. Fold half of the dry ingredients into the butter mixture. Mix in the milk and buttermilk, then the rest of the dry ingredients. Fold in the coconut.

3 Using a piping (pastry) bag fitted with a large plain nozzle, pipe 12 5cm/ 2in rounds of cake mixture (batter) 5cm/2in apart on each baking tray. Bake, in batches, for 12–15 minutes, or until the cakes bounce back when pressed. Transfer to a wire rack to cool.

4 For the filling, put the egg whites and sugar in a heatproof bowl and place the bowl over a pan of gently simmering water. Using an electric whisk, whisk the ingredients together until the sugar has dissolved and the mixture is white and hot.

5 Remove the bowl from the heat and continue to whisk on high speed until the bottom of the bowl starts to cool down. Turn the speed down to low and whisk in the butter, a little at a time.

6 Fold in the lemon rind and juice and lemon extract.

7 To make the icing, mix the icing sugar and lemon juice together in a small bowl to form a smooth paste.

8 To assemble the pies, using a piping bag fitted with a star-shaped nozzle, pipe a round of lemon filling on to the flat side of one cake and top with the flat side of another. Repeat to make 24 pies.

9 Spread a little icing over the top of each pie and immediately sprinkle with coconut. Refrigerate the pies until you are ready to arrange and serve them (2–3 hours will allow the filling to firm up).

10 Pile the whoopie pies on top of each other to form a pyramid-shaped stack. Sprinkle with pink rose petals.

Nutritional information: Energy 522kcal/2197kJ; Protein 5g; Carbohydrate 57g, of which sugars 37g; Fat 32g, of which saturates 22g; Cholesterol 90mg; Calcium 73mg; Fibre 3.1g; Sodium 340mg.